Rebekah Kassim
03/17/18

UNDUE OVERFLOW

52 Devotionals for Breakthrough into Supernatural Abundance

Rebekah Kassim

ISBN: 1530930340
ISBN 13: 9781530930340
Library of Congress Control Number: 2017900676
CreateSpace Independent Publishing Platform
North Charleston, South Carolina
Unless otherwise stated, all Bible verses are from the New King James
Version (NKJV).

DEDICATION

I dedicate this book to the Lord Jesus Christ, the Author and Finisher of my faith. Dear Lord, thank you for lending me your pen to write this book; let your word be confirmed with signs and wonders in the lives of the readers. Amen.

CONTENTS

ACKNOWLEDGEMENTS

I am indebted to Nellie Joy Dagoon for her rigorous and painstaking editing of the manuscript, and for her invaluable suggestions and professional advice. I would like to thank my amazing husband, Mark, for his unwavering support and partnership; and my five magnificent children, Eni, Tobi, Ogo, Dotun, and Simi for always being a great source of joy and inspiration to me.

Blessings!!!

Rebekah

INTRODUCTION

On Monday, February 13th, 2017, Lake Oroville Dam in Sacramento overflowed its banks for the first time in 50 years causing an evacuation order of 200,000 people who lived downstream. As I watched the overflowing waters rush down the spillway on TV, I saw the closest image to what the Lord laid on my heart about UNDUE OVERFLOW. On October 7, 2014, during my morning devotion, I had a vision of this book with the cover and the title: "Undue Overflow -- 52 Devotionals." I looked up the meaning of *Undue*, and I got excited just thinking about the combination of these two powerful words! Undue means excessive, extravagant, lavish and too much. Overflow already means that there is more than enough. Therefore, undue overflow is excessive, extravagant, lavish or too much overflow.

*Now to him who is able to do **exceedingly abundantly above** all that we ask or think, according to the power that works in us, to him be glory in the church by Christ Jesus to all generations, forever and ever. Amen.*

--Ephesians 3:20-21

You prepare a table before me in the presence of my enemies.
You have anointed and refreshed my head with oil;
*My cup **overflows.***

--Psalm 23:5 AMP

It is interesting that at the time the Lord gave me this revelation, my husband and I were going through the worst fiscal crisis of our lives. My husband had just come out of a business partnership that went awry. He needed to pay up employees and suppliers, fold up that business as it then was, and start something new all over again. In the physical realm, it was a dire situation, but in the spiritual realm, the Lord was telling us that he was taking us to a place of not only more than enough, but a place of excessively more than enough! I am happy to report that God has watched over his word to perform it. Within two short years, the Lord re-established our business on a new foundation, all the debts were paid, and in the place where we barely survived, we began to prosper. All that change was happening as I wrote this book. Every time we made remarkable progress, I was reminded that the promise of *Undue Overflow* is true.

If *Undue Overflow* is God's will for our lives, then why are we not experiencing the abundance of all things? In the book, I discuss the hindrances to overflow and how to avoid them. The hindrances are like blockages in the pipeline of our supplies, when the blockages are removed, the supplies will flow freely without interruption. This book is designed to be used over the course of a year. There are 52 devotionals that could be read daily or weekly at the reader's convenience. I have included questions for reflection, and bible verses for meditation and memorization at the end of each devotional. It is my hope and prayer that as you use this book, your mind will be transformed. May all hindrances to your prosperity be removed, so that your capacity for increase is enlarged.

I therefore invite you to dinner with the King of Kings. Welcome to the banquet! He has set a table before you in the presence your enemies! He anoints your head with oil. Your cup OVERFLOWS!

Rebekah Kassim

OTHER BIBLE TRANSLATIONS AND ABBREVIATIONS

Amplified Bible - **AMP**
English Standard Version - **ESV**
Lexham English Bible - **LEB**
The Message - **MSG**
New International Version - **NIV**
Living Bible - **TLB**

UNDUE- DICTIONARY MEANINGS

Undue; Exceeding a normal or reasonable limit: (The Free Dictionary).

Synonyms
excessive, exorbitant, extravagant, extreme, immoderate, inordinate, overabundant, overmuch.

The American Heritage® Roget's Thesaurus. Copyright © 2013, 2014 by Houghton Mifflin Harcourt Publishing Company. Published by Houghton Mifflin Harcourt Publishing Company

PART I
GOD'S IDEA OF OVERFLOW

God's Idea of overflow is way beyond our imagination. God thinks exponentially and infinitely. The bible says his thoughts are far from ours as the heavens are far from the earth (Isaiah 55:9). A thousand years are like a day in his sight (Psalms 90:4). His good thoughts towards us are like the sands on the sea, they cannot be numbered (Psalms 139:17-18).

God's thoughts about overflow are higher than we can fathom, so we need to prepare our hearts to receive the blessings he has for us. We need to make room by digging wells in our spirits and allowing him to fill our wells with water. How do we dig wells? By meditating on his word, until we receive understanding in our hearts. When we receive understanding, the word becomes flesh. Then we can experience the promise accordingly as God has purposed.

God's idea of overflow is **undue**, and excessive, such that we need to wrap our minds around it to be able to experience it. In the next few devotionals we will unwrap the gift of overflow of blessings according to the promises of God.

CHAPTER 1

UNDUE OVERFLOW

Now to him who is able to do exceedingly abundantly
above all that we ask or think, according to the power
that works in us, to him be glory in the church by Christ
Jesus to all generations, forever and ever. Amen.

Ephesians 3:20-21

The apostle Paul, in speaking to the Ephesians could not find the right words to express how great God's love towards us is, so he tried to describe it in poetic superlative language --*exceedingly, abundantly above*, is another way of saying abundant overflow, excessive overflow, and way more above whatever exponential infinite overflow may mean to you.

When we begin to believe the magnitude and the size of the overflow that God has in mind for us, then our expectations of what God has in store for us, and what he planned for our lives will change. To experience the blessings of God at this level, we need to tap into the power that works within us. This is the resurrection power that raised Jesus from the dead; the same power is at work in us to bring us into this glorious experience.

In other words, the overflowing blessings that we are talking about in this book are for those who have trusted Jesus as their personal Lord and Savior, and thus have access to the power of the Holy Spirit living inside of them. There is a supernatural dimension of supplies that God wants to bring us into. As we study the word of God, we can begin to receive illumination in our spirit man, so that the resurrection power in us can bring us into the fullness of all that God has purposed for our lives.

Questions for Reflection

1. Are you experiencing God's overflowing blessings in every area of your life?
2. Are you experiencing overflowing blessings in your finances and materially?
3. What would your life look like if you were experiencing overflow in every area of your life?
4. What would your life look like if you were experiencing financial overflow?

Meditate

But as it is written: "Eye has not seen, nor ear heard, nor have entered into the heart of man the things which God has prepared for those who love him." But God has revealed them to us through his Spirit. For the Spirit searches all things, yes, the deep things of God.

--1 Corinthians 2:9-10

Memory Verse

He who did not spare his own Son, but delivered him up for us all, how shall he not with him also freely give us all things?

--Romans 8:32

Prayer

Dear Lord,
I thank you for your resurrection power that is at work in me. Unlock my imagination so that I can receive in my mind and spirit the magnitude of your plans to bless me. Amen.

CHAPTER 2
BLESSINGS INTENDED

Let them shout for joy and be glad, who
favor my righteous cause; and let them say
continually, "Let the Lord be magnified, who has
pleasure in the prosperity of his servant."

Psalms 35:27

P salm 35 was David's lamentation for all the woes that befell
him, especially in his relationships. The people that he trusted
were the ones who wanted to destroy him. In this psalm, he poured
out to God the bitterness of his soul, asking for God's intervention
and protection on his life. Interestingly, at the end of the psalm,
he switched tones, and started thanking God for his prosperity. He
reassured himself that God delighted in his prosperity regardless
of the ill will of his enemies. David was convinced that God's plan
was for him to prosper; he was not going to let his enemies' threats
remove that hope from him.

We need to know in the depths of our inner beings that God wants to bless us.

Beloved, I pray that you may prosper in all things and be in health, just as your soul prospers.

--3 John 2

It is very important that we understand that it is God's will to bless us. The Lord delights in our prosperity just like we delight in the prosperity of our children. The devil may tempt us with adversity, poverty and lack, but if we keep our confession, the enemy will eventually back off, and we will enter the fullness of the blessings God has promised us.

David kept confessing the goodness of God despite his circumstances. He was handsomely rewarded with wealth and riches after his trials.

Blessed be the Lord, who daily loads us with benefits, the God of our salvation!

--Psalms 68:19

God the father made provision for our salvation through the death of Jesus Christ, so that we can enjoy a daily load of his blessings in our lives. Prosperity is the birthright of every believer in Jesus Christ.

Questions for Reflection

1. Do you believe that it is God's will to bless you abundantly?
2. Does your present circumstance reflect this belief?
3. Are you more comfortable with the thought that God wants you to be poor?
4. Are there some thought patterns that you need to change so that you can receive the fullness of God's blessing?
5. What does "an overload of benefits" mean to you?

Meditation

The rich man's wealth is his strong city; the destruction of the poor is their poverty.

--Proverbs 10:15

Memory Verse

And you shall remember the Lord your God, for it is he who gives you power to get wealth; that he may establish his covenant which he swore to your fathers, as it is this day.

--Deuteronomy 8:18

Prayer

Dear Lord,

Help me to receive your promise of blessings for my life. I ask that you strengthen me by your power in my inner man. Let me not be moved by any lie of the enemy to convince me against your blessings for my life. I believe your word that you want me blessed. Amen.

CHAPTER 3

RENEW YOUR MIND

*And do not be conformed to this world, but be transformed
by the renewing of your mind, that you may prove what
is that good, and acceptable, and perfect will of God.*

Romans. 12:2

O ur minds sometimes do not want to do the will of God. Our
flesh, imaginations, old ideas and cultural beliefs die hard.
We need to re-train our minds with the word of God. Any area
of our lives that is not in alignment with the revealed will of God
needs to be transformed. However, if we do not study the word of
God, and take time to meditate on it, we would be living below
God's plan for our lives and not even realize it. God wants us to
overflow in abundance, but if we grew up in poverty, or in a culture that suggested that it is not spiritual to be wealthy, our minds
would reject God's offer of overflow before we unwrap the gift.

We need to train our minds not to murmur and complain when
we come into God's presence. God offered the children of Israel

a land that flowed with milk and honey, but the inconvenience of their wilderness journey beclouded their vision. They could not see beyond their immediate circumstance, therefore they rejected the offer and turned back from the promise. Train your heart to overflow with God's promises rather than with "heart murmurs." Then you will experience the overflow of the promised land.

If you are willing and obedient, you shall eat the good of the land.

--Isaiah. 1:19

Questions for Reflection

1. In what areas of your life have you experienced the efficacy of the word of God?
2. In what areas are you not experiencing the efficacy of the word of God?
3. Do you have a specific testimony of how you applied the word of God in a circumstance and how it worked for you?
4. Do you remember a time that God supplied your needs supernaturally?
5. Do you know anyone who has a testimony of supernatural healing?
6. Do you know anyone who has a testimony of financial breakthrough?
7. How did the word of God work in both circumstances?

Meditation

Blessed is the man who walks not in the counsel of the ungodly, nor stands in the path of sinners, nor sits in the seat of the scornful; But his delight is in the law of the Lord, and in his law, he meditates day and night. He shall be like a tree planted by the rivers of water; that brings forth its fruit in its season, whose leaf also shall not wither; and whatever he does shall prosper.

-- Psalms. 1:1-3

Memory Verse

This book of the Law shall not depart from your mouth, but you shall meditate in it day and night, that you may observe to do according to all that is written in it. For then you will make your way prosperous, and then you will have good success.

--Joshua. 1:8

Prayer

Dear Lord,

Help me to be a student of your word. Help me to meditate on it day and night so that I can make my way prosperous. In your name, I pray. Amen.

CHAPTER 4

EXPONENTIAL BLESSINGS

*Now it shall come to pass, if you diligently obey the
voice of the Lord your God, to observe carefully all
His commandments which I command you today,
that the Lord your God will set you high above
all nations of the earth. And all these blessings
shall come upon you and overtake you, because
you obey the voice of the Lord your God:
Blessed shall you be in the city, and
blessed shall you be in the country.
Blessed shall be the fruit of your body, the produce of
your ground and the increase of your herds, the increase
of your cattle and the offspring of your flocks.
Blessed shall be your basket and your kneading bowl.
Blessed shall you be when you come in, and
blessed shall you be when you go out.
The Lord will cause your enemies who rise against
you to be defeated before your face; they shall come out
against you one way and flee before you seven ways.
The Lord will command the blessing on you
in your storehouses and in all to which you set*

*your hand, and He will bless you in the land
which the Lord your God is giving you.
The Lord will establish you as a holy people to
Himself, just as He has sworn to you, if you keep the
commandments of the Lord your God and walk in His
ways. Then all peoples of the earth shall see that you are
called by the name of the Lord, and they shall be afraid
of you. And the Lord will grant you plenty of goods, in
the fruit of your body, in the increase of your livestock,
and in the produce of your ground, in the land of which
the Lord swore to your fathers to give you. The Lord
will open to you His good treasure, the heavens, to give
the rain to your land in its season, and to bless all the
work of your hand. You shall lend to many nations,
but you shall not borrow. And the Lord will make you
the head and not the tail; you shall be above only, and
not be beneath, if you heed the commandments of the
Lord your God, which I command you today, and are
careful to observe them. So, you shall not turn aside
from any of the words which I command you this day, to
the right or the left, to go after other gods to serve them.*

Deuteronomy 28:1-14

Questions for Reflection

1. After reading and meditating on Deuteronomy 28: 1-14, do you think these promises are "too good to be true?"
2. Do you think that you qualify for these blessings?
3. What is the ONLY condition you need to fulfill for these blessings to operate in your life? (Hint- Obedience to God).
4. Are you experiencing the manifestation of these blessings?
5. If not, why do you think you are not fully enjoying these promises?

Meditation

The blessing of the Lord makes one rich, and he adds no sorrow with it.

--Proverbs 10:22

Memory Verse

If they obey and serve him, they shall spend their days in prosperity, and their years in pleasures.

--Job 36:11

Prayer

Father God,
Thank you for your promise to bless me. Help me to obey you in all things. Let your blessings come upon me and overtake me, in Jesus name, Amen.

CHAPTER 5

OVERFLOWING CUP

*You prepare a table before me in the presence of
my enemies. You have anointed and refreshed
my head with oil; my cup overflows.*

Psalm 23:5 (AMP)

I had a three-part vision early one morning in the course of writing this book. First, I saw a row of tiny cylindrical silver cups, then I saw a hand carrying a dainty bottle of golden liquid which I thought was perfume. The hand then poured all the contents of the bottle into one of the silver cups. The golden perfume filled the cup and ***overflowed***; the perfume was obviously too much for the cup. Then I asked in my mind, "What kind of perfume is this?"

The vision continued. I saw myself eating a richly filled ham sandwich, and then finally, I saw myself drinking an orange colored fizzy drink from a bottle. The vision stopped and the Lord spoke to my heart, "I set a table before you in the presence of your enemies. I anointed your head with oil; your cup overflows."   I realized that the golden liquid in the bottle was anointing oil and not just ordinary perfume as I had imagined, because anointing oil has its own unique fragrance.

The Lord played a visual of the fifth verse of the twenty-third psalm for me, and I could imagine the extent to which our cups should be overflowing. The silver cup was drenched with the oil and the oil flowed down both sides of the cup to the surroundings in a way that looked like a 'waste' of oil, but the excess was intentional. When the blessings of God overflow in our lives, it goes out to all in our sphere of influence. Everywhere we go, God wants us to be channels of his blessings to other people.

Questions for Reflection

1. Psalm 23 is an all-time favorite for Christians. Can you recite the psalm?
2. How have you experienced the Lord as your shepherd?
3. Has he truly not allowed you to be in want?
4. Who or what are the enemies you think the psalmist referred to in verse 5? (Hint: lack, poverty, and infirmity).
5. Why does God want your cup to overflow?

Meditation

The Lord is my Shepherd [to feed, to guide and to shield me],
I shall not want.
He lets me lie down in green pastures;
He leads me beside the still and quiet waters.
He refreshes and restores my soul (life);
He leads me in the paths of righteousness
for his name's sake.
Even though I walk through the [sunless] valley of the shadow of death, I fear no evil, for you are with me;
Your rod [to protect] and your staff [to guide], they comfort and console me.
You prepare a table before me in the presence of my enemies.
You have anointed and refreshed my head with oil;
My cup overflows.
Surely goodness and mercy and unfailing love shall follow me all the days of my life, and I shall dwell forever [throughout all my days] in the house and in the presence of the Lord.

--Psalm 23 (AMP)

Memory Verse

You prepare a table before me in the presence of my enemies.
You have anointed and refreshed my head with oil;
My cup overflows.

--Psalm 23:5

Prayers

Dear Lord,
*   Enlarge my vision. Prepare me for the overflow. Bless me and make me a blessing to my generations, in Jesus name. Amen.*

CHAPTER 6
ABUNDANT SATISFACTION

How precious is your loving kindness, O God!
Therefore, the children of men put their trust under
the shadow of your wings. They are abundantly
satisfied with the fullness of your house, and you
give them drink from the river of your pleasures.

Psalms 36:7-8

I love Psalm 36! This psalm reveals the tender heart of God towards us. When we put our trust in God, he brings us into his banqueting hall and fills us with all manner of good things. He plays the host, invites us to dinner and feeds us with sumptuous delicacies until we are "abundantly satisfied." Then he starts serving the finest of drinks. We could have whatever we want from *the River of His Pleasures*. This is a revelation of how much God wants to bless his children.

Moses bestowed this type of blessings on the tribe of Naphthali;

O Naphtali, satisfied with favor, and full with the blessing of the Lord, possess thou the west and the south.

--Deuteronomy 33:23

Again, we see the word "satisfied" in this verse. When God favors you, you will automatically be blessed. Being blessed is a by-product of his favor. However, we do not want to experience sporadic favor from God. We need to ask for abundant satisfaction so that we are never short on his blessings.

Abundance of God's favor culminating in the possession of lands was a priest's blessing on one of the twelve tribes of Israel. If Moses, an earthly leader could pray this prayer for his followers, we too can ask our heavenly Father for favor to possess lands and territories.

Questions for Reflection

1. Have you ever attended a state dinner or a sumptuous buffet at a palatial restaurant?
2. How much would you eat?
3. Would you leave the place hungry?
4. What if you could take some food with you after the dinner due to excess food, what would you do?
5. Imagine yourself at God's banqueting table?
6. What Psalm comes to your mind? (Hint; Psalms 23 and 36).

Meditation

For the Lord God is a sun and shield: The Lord will give grace and glory: no good thing will he withhold from those who walk uprightly.

-- Psalms 84:1

Memory Verse

He brought me to the banqueting house, and his banner over me was love.

--Song of Solomon 2:4

Prayer

Lord,
I thank you for the goodness that you have prepared for me as I seek your face. I am a vessel of honor; I lift my cup. Fill me with abundance of your goodness. Amen.

CHAPTER 7

YEAR-ROUND BLESSINGS

You crown the year with your goodness, and
your paths drip with abundance.

Psalms 65:11

God wants to bless us from the beginning of the year to the end. He wants our year to start, and end with his goodness and abundance. He also longs to bless us all the way in-between as we walk in his paths. All year round, God makes all things to work together for our maximum productivity. The daily cycles and seasons all work together in harmony to create an atmosphere conducive for the fruitfulness of all manner of produce.

The farmer prepares the soil, plants the seeds, makes ridges, and waters the furrows. Then, the Lord brings the increase. This process can be likened to the work of our hands, our jobs, our businesses, and other sources of income. As we go about performing the work of our hands, we should be expectant of God's favor -- daily, weekly, monthly, and yearly.

At the end of one year, and the beginning of a new year, we should be recording a higher level of increase than we did in the previous year. This is the will of God for us. He wants to CROWN our efforts with good success every year. As we follow his paths in obedience, we begin to experience increase all year round, all the days of our lives.

But the path of the just is as the shining light, that shines more and more to the perfect day.

--Proverbs 4:18

Questions for Reflection

1. Have you ever been directly involved in a natural planting process?
2. Do you enjoy gardening?
3. After preparing the soil, planting the seeds and watering them, what else did you have to do for the plant to grow? (Hint: water the plant)
4. When you planted the seeds in their season, did you get a good harvest?
5. What was your response when you saw the fruits of your gardening efforts?
6. Would you have reaped a harvest if you had not sown seed?

Meditation

A land for which the Lord your God cares; the eyes of the Lord your God are always on it, from the beginning of the year to the very end of the year. Then I will give you the rain for your land in its season, the early rain and the latter rain, that you may gather in your grain, your new wine, and your oil.

--Deuteronomy 11:12-14

Memory Verse

And let the beauty of the Lord our God be upon us, and establish the work of our hands for us; Yes, establish the work of our hands.

--Psalms. 90:17

Prayers

Lord Jesus,

Make my life your garden. Let every part of my life blossom with your glory and beauty. Make me a fruitful branch of your vine. Amen.

CHAPTER 8

BLESSINGS REVEALED

But as it is written: "Eye has not seen, nor ear heard,
nor have entered into the heart of man, the things
which God has prepared for those who love him." But
God has revealed them to us through his Spirit. For the
Spirit searches all things, yes, the deep things of God.

1 Corinthians 2:9-10

The blessing of the Lord makes one rich,
and he adds no sorrow with it.

Proverbs. 10:22

God's purpose for blessing his people is to make us rich and fulfilled. The blessing of the Lord is an expression of his goodwill to us. He is plenteous in mercy and full of loving kindness. Just as we long to bless our children with all manner of good things, the Lord longs to bless us because he loves us. The blessing he has prepared for everyone is unique and specific, it may not be obvious to other people.

However, the born-again believer has the advantage of the Spirit of God dwelling on the inside to reveal the things that God has prepared for him. The bible says,

> *It is the glory of God to conceal a matter, but the glory of kings is to search out a matter.*

--Proverbs. 25:2

We have the honor and responsibility to seek the Lord and inquire of him, so that his spirit can reveal to us the blessings that he has prepared for us, our spouses, children, and descendants. When we begin to implement his instructions, and directions, then we will see the blessings begin to manifest in our situation and circumstance.

Questions for Reflection

1. Have you asked Jesus Christ into your heart?
2. If not, would you like to do so now?
3. Do you believe that Jesus Christ died on the cross for your sins?
4. Do you believe that he rose on the third day for your justification?

Confess your belief according to Romans 10:9-10:

> If *you confess with your mouth the Lord Jesus and believe in your heart that God has raised him from the dead, you will be saved. For with the heart one believes unto righteousness, and with the mouth confession is made unto salvation.*

If you asked Jesus to come into your heart, you just made the greatest decision of your life. CONGRATULATIONS!

Meditation

> *The secret things belong to the Lord our God, but those things which are revealed belong to us and to our children forever, that we may do all the words of this law.*
>
> --Deuteronomy. 29:29

Memory Verse

> *I will give you the treasures of darkness, and hidden riches of secret places, that you may know that I, the Lord, who call you by your name, Am the God of Israel.*
>
> --Isaiah 45:3

Prayers

Dear Lord,
I pray that you reveal to my spirit your plans for my prosperity,
and order my feet in the paths of blessedness, in Jesus' name. Amen.

PART II
GENERATIONAL BLESSINGS

I n the next few devotionals, we will examine how God promised to bless one man and through him, bless all generations in the earth. Abraham's blessing was passed from his son Isaac to the children of Israel, and from the children of Israel to whosoever believes in Jesus.

> *Get out of your country, from your family, and from your father's house, to a land that I will show you. I will make you a great nation; **I will bless you**, and make your name great; and you* shall be a blessing. *I will **bless** those who **bless** you, and I will curse him who curses you; and in you all the families of the earth shall be **blessed**."*

> --Genesis 12:1-3

When we become born again, we gain access into the Abrahamic blessings by our salvation.

> *And he received the sign of circumcision, a seal of the righteousness of the faith which he had while still uncircumcised, that he might be*

the father of all those who believe, though they are uncircumcised, that righteousness might be imputed to them also.

--Romans 4:11

The Abrahamic blessing was a promise of increase and greatness for Abraham and his descendants. We would see in this section how the blessing was transferred from Abraham to the Jews and eventually to us when we get saved.

CHAPTER 9

THE BLESSING OF ABRAHAM

Now the Lord had said to Abram: "Get out of your country, from your family, and from your father's house, to a land that I will show you." I will make you a great nation; I will bless you, and make your name great; and you shall be a blessing. I will bless those who bless you, and I will curse him who curses you; and in you all the families of the earth shall be blessed."

Genesis 12:1-3

God had a grand plan to bless all the families of the earth. He chose to start from one man, Abraham. God called Abraham out of a pagan culture and promised to bless him. Abraham had not done anything to prove his faith in God when God chose to bless him. The blessing came with the call. Abraham could inherit the blessing when he responded to God by faith.

God blessed Abraham as he promised, and also blessed his descendants, who eventually became the nation of Israel. We received the gift of Jesus Christ through the nation of Israel. Jesus died on the cross, so that Jews and Gentiles might be saved. The Apostle Paul explained this in Galatians.

And the scripture, foreseeing that God would justify the Gentiles by faith, preached the gospel to Abraham beforehand, saying, "In you all the nations shall be blessed." So, then those who are of faith are blessed with believing Abraham.

--Galatians. 3:8-9 (ESV)

Christ has redeemed us from the curse of the law, having become a curse for us (for it is written, "Cursed is everyone who hangs on a tree"), that the blessing of Abraham might come upon the Gentiles in Christ Jesus, that we might receive the promise of the Spirit through faith.

--Galatians. 3:13-14

When we trusted Jesus as our Lord and Savior, not only were our sins forgiven, we also entered the Abrahamic covenant of blessings -- we gain access into a covenant of wealth because the curse of poverty was broken at the cross. Amen.

Questions for Reflection

1. Do you '*see*' yourself as a partaker of the Abrahamic covenant?
2. Did God's call of Abraham sound like the gospel to you? (Hint-- Galatians. 3:8).
3. God called Abraham and blessed him just for answering the call. How does that relate to the call you received at salvation?
4. After studying this devotional, do you now see yourself positioned for the blessing as a descendant of Abraham?

Meditation

And you shall remember the Lord your God, for it is he who gives you power to get wealth, that he may establish his covenant which he swore to your fathers, as it is this day.

--Deuteronomy 8:18

Memory Verse

And if you are Christ's, then you are Abraham's seed, and heirs according to the promise.

--Psalm 105:8-10

Prayer

Dear Lord,
Thank you for making provision for my prosperity through your covenant with Abraham. I confess with my mouth that I am Abraham's seed, and therefore I have full access to my inheritance in Jesus' name. Amen.

CHAPTER 10

ISAAC- BLESSED IN A RECESSION

*Then Isaac sowed in that land, and reaped in the
same year a hundredfold; and the Lord blessed him.
The man began to prosper, and continued prospering
until he became very prosperous; for he had possessions
of flocks and possessions of herds and a great number
of servants. So, the Philistines envied him.*

Genesis 26:12-14

I saac lived in Gerar, the land of the Philistines. He had inherited his father's estate but the enemy wanted to run him out of
his inheritance. There was a severe famine in the land; therefore.
Isaac decided to go down to Egypt, just like his father Abraham
did when he encountered a famine (Genesis 12:10). But God had
a different plan.

God appeared to Isaac. He reminded Isaac of his covenant of blessing with Abraham. God told Isaac not to leave Gerar, because he was planning to show himself strong on Isaac's behalf. God promised to bless him despite the drought, and he did! He blessed Isaac supernaturally. Isaac sowed in Gerar in the time of famine and he had a bounteous harvest that year. His success was resounding because his business was the only one spared from the drought that year. Isaac became the wealthiest man in the land, and he continued to increase in wealth.

These days, many nations are in the throes of economic recession. Even the United States is just recovering from the great recession. It does not matter where you live, or the economic situation of your nation; God wants to bless and increase you. He makes a way where there seems to be no way; he brings streams in the desert (Isaiah 43:19).

Questions for Reflection

1. Have you ever lived in a recession?
2. Can you remember how God supernaturally supplied your needs?
3. Do you believe that he can do it again?

Meditation

Do not remember the former things, nor consider the things of old. Behold, I will do a new thing, now it shall spring forth; shall you not know it? I will even make a road in the wilderness and rivers in the desert.

--Isaiah 43:18-19

Memory Verse

The Lord knows the days of the upright, and their inheritance shall be forever. They shall not be ashamed in the evil time, and in the days of famine they shall be satisfied.

--Psalm 37:18-19

Prayer

Dear Lord,

I thank you that you are my great provider. Thank you for turning my finances around for good. I refuse to participate in any recession. I choose supernatural supplies and abundance for me and my household in Jesus' name. Amen.

CHAPTER 11

JACOB- BLESSED BY REVELATION

"And it happened, at the time when the flocks conceived,
that I lifted my eyes and saw in a dream, and behold, the
rams which leaped upon the flocks were streaked, speckled,
and gray-spotted. Then the Angel of God spoke to me
in a dream, saying, 'Jacob.' And I said, 'Here I am.'

Genesis 31:10-11

Jacob was next in line for the blessing. Isaac was tricked by Rebekah and Jacob to pass the blessing to Jacob instead of his elderly brother Esau. Esau threatened to kill him, so he ran for his life. On his way to his uncle Laban's house, Jacob started having dreams and visions of God and his angels. This would become an important and recurrent feature in his life. Jacob lived with Laban for 20 years, married two of his daughters, and tended his sheep. Laban, however, was a mean employer; he changed Jacob's wages ten times! Despite that, the Lord prospered Jacob, contrary to Laban's expectations.

In another dream, the Lord revealed to Jacob the strategy for multiplication. The angel of the Lord instructed him on how to mate the animals such that all the strong animals became Jacob's.

And the man increased exceedingly, and had much cattle, and maidservants, and menservants, and camels, and asses.

-- Genesis 30:43

Laban was not happy that Jacob was blessed, but he could not stop the covenant of blessing that was on Jacob's life. Jacob left Laban and went back to Canaan a very wealthy man. The covenant of blessing is also at work in your life, but you need to co-operate with your angels. God can give you too business ideas, and strategies that will make you prosperous. As you step out by faith, to obey his leading, you will find yourself on the pathway to prosperity.

Questions for Reflection

1. Do you believe in dreams and visions?
2. If not, why?
3. Do you expect God to speak to you through dreams and visions?
4. Have you ever received direction from the spirit of God through a dream or vision?
5. Did you follow through with the direction after you woke up?
6. What was the result of the steps of faith you took after your dream?
7. Do you know of other people in the bible who had dreams and visions?

Meditation

And it shall come to pass afterward, that I will pour out my spirit on all flesh; and your sons and your daughters shall prophesy, your old men shall dream dreams, your young men shall see visions.

--Joel 2:28

Memory Verse

Now a word was secretly brought to me, and my ear received a whisper of it; in disquieting thoughts from the visions of the night, when deep sleep falls on men.

--Job 4:12-13

Prayer

Lord,

Open the eyes of my heart so that I might see you both day and night. Grant me wisdom to understand the messages you are sending to me by your Spirit. Amen.

CHAPTER 12
JOSEPH- BLESSED BEYOND MEASURE

*Now Joseph was governor over the land; and it was
he who sold to all the people of the land. And Joseph's
brothers came and bowed down before him with
their faces to the earth... Then Joseph remembered
the dreams which he had dreamed about them.*

Genesis 42:6, 9a

There is a little change in the dynamics of the transference of the Abrahamic blessing at this point. Jacob had twelve sons, the eldest of which should have rightfully received the inheritance. But God had a grander plan. The blessing would be passed to the least likely -- a dreamer! Joseph was Jacob's eleventh child, dearly beloved by his father. In addition to this, he started having grandiose dreams about ruling over his brothers. His dreams got him into trouble. His brothers sold him into slavery in the land of

Egypt. Through a series of divinely orchestrated circumstances, from slavery to prison, and from prison to Pharaoh's palace, God brought Joseph's dream to pass.

Joseph became the prime minister for food and finances in the land of Egypt during a time of severe famine all over the earth. Joseph's dreams came to pass when he had the opportunity to feed his brothers in the time of famine and to eventually relocate his whole family to the land of Egypt so that the family escaped the famine, and prospered. Therefore, through Joseph, the Abrahamic blessing was passed on to the Israelites. Sometimes when God puts a dream in our hearts, it is to increase us so that others may be blessed through us. Even if it looks like the dream will not come to pass, we need to endure, so that we can obtain the promise.

Hold fast your profession, because he is faithful that promised.

--Hebrews 10:23

He that started a great work in you will bring it to complete fruition in the day of our Lord Jesus Christ. Amen.

--Philippians 1:6.

Questions for Reflection

1. Has God given you a promise that has not yet happened?
2. Do you have dreams, or ideas in your heart that you feel are too big for you to accomplish?
3. Have you started working on a project and stopped because you got discouraged?
4. Joseph's story is an example of how God can bring his will to pass despite difficult circumstances. Were you encouraged by his story?
5. Will you go back and start working on what God has put in your or heart, and continue the project you abandoned?

Meditation

But as for you, you meant evil against me; but God meant it for good, in order to bring it about as it is this day, to save many people alive.

--Genesis 50:20

Memory Verse

And we know that all things work together for good to those who love God, to those who are called according to his purpose.

--Romans 8:28

Prayer

Dear Lord,
Grant me the grace to be patient in my walk with you. Help me to wait for your deliverance and intervention in my circumstance. Help me to be faithful until I receive the promises you have given me. Amen.

CHAPTER 13

THE ISRAELITES – PLUNDERED THE ENEMY

*"Know certainly that your descendants will be
strangers in a land that is not theirs, and will serve
them, and they will afflict them four hundred years.
And also, the nation whom they serve I will judge;
afterward they shall come out with great possessions.*

Genesis 15:13-14

When God cut a covenant with Abraham, he revealed to him that he would bless Abraham's descendants through a nation whom they will serve. The Abrahamic blessing is now about to be transferred from the twelve sons of Jacob to the nation of Israel. The transformation from a clan to nation occurred over a period of 400 years. When God called Moses to deliver the children of Israel, he reiterated this promise.

I will give this people favor in the sight of the Egyptians; and it shall be, when you go, that you shall not go empty-handed. But every woman shall ask of her neighbor, namely, of her who dwells near her house, articles of silver, articles of gold, and clothing; and you shall put them on your sons and on your daughters. So, you shall plunder the Egyptians.

--Exodus 3:21-22

According to the verse below, God watched over his word in the lives of Abraham's descendants to perform it.

Now the children of Israel had done according to the word of Moses, and they had asked from the Egyptians articles of silver, articles of gold, and clothing. And the Lord had given the people favor in the sight of the Egyptians, so that they granted them what they requested. Thus, they plundered the Egyptians.

--Exodus 12:35-36

The children of Israel, the descendants of Abraham, inherited the blessing that God promised Abraham. The same blessing has been extended to us through our faith in Jesus Christ. We are joint heirs with Christ and partakers of the Abrahamic blessing. Blessed be the name of the Lord forever. Hallelujah!

Questions for Reflection

1. After studying the transference of the blessing in the past few devotionals, do you see yourself positioned for the blessing?
2. Christ has redeemed us from the curse of the law. Do you know that poverty and lack are curses?
3. Christ became poor so that we may be rich. Why should we continue in poverty?
4. Are you able to now freely receive the promise of the blessing of the Lord? If we believe in our hearts that Jesus rose from the dead and confess with our mouth, we shall be saved. Similarly, if we believe in our hearts that God wants us to be blessed and we confess with our mouth that we are rich, we shall be blessed.

Meditation

He brought them forth also with silver and gold: and there was not one feeble person among their tribes.

--Psalm 105:37

Memory Verse

The rich man's wealth is his strong city; the destruction of the poor is their poverty.

--Proverbs 10:15

Prayer

Lord,

I thank you because you will not withhold anything good from me. Christ has redeemed me from the curse of poverty, and therefore, I break every agreement with the spirit of shortage and lack. I choose life and I choose blessings. I decree that the blessings of Abraham are mine in Jesus' name. Amen.

PART III

FROM FAMINE TO PLENTY

The Israelites inherited the blessing of Abraham, but they were not always diligent to maintain the level of blessedness that God desired for them. Anytime the Israelites were disobedient to God, they found themselves on the other side of the blessing: famine. However, when they returned to God, the Lord would intervene in their circumstance. In the next few devotionals, we would examine how God miraculously supplied the needs of his chosen people.

CHAPTER 14

THE WIDOW OF ZAREPATH

And Elijah said to her, "Do not fear; go and do as you
have said, but make me a small cake from it first, and
bring it to me; and afterward make some for yourself and
your son. For thus says the Lord God of Israel: 'The bin
of flour shall not be used up, nor shall the jar of oil run
dry, until the day the Lord sends rain on the earth.'" So,
she went away and did according to the word of Elijah;
and she and he and her household ate for many days.

I Kings 17:13-15

Ahab was a wicked King who led the children of Israel into sin and idolatry. The Lord was so angry with the nation that he prompted Elijah the prophet of God to decree that there would be no rain in the land of Israel for three years. A severe famine ensued. In the early days of the famine, the Lord had ravens bring food to Elijah while he lived by brook Cherinth. After many days, the brook dried up and Elijah needed a new place of supplies. The Lord then sent Elijah to a widow in the city of Zarepath.

Elijah asked her for water, which already was a scarce commodity. She, however, proceeded to give him water, and Elijah did the unthinkable thing! He asked the widow for cake, which would be like asking for lunch. The widow then explained the severity of the famine to the prophet. She was on her last measure of flour and oil; she was planning to feed herself and her son for the last time, and then wait to die of starvation. That was a hopeless situation.

However, it was God's will for the widow to live. So, Elijah prophesied to her that she would never run out of flour and oil. As she cooked what was supposed to be the last meal, the flour and oil increased and multiplied! Because of this miracle, the widow, her household, and Elijah had food for many days. You may be in a seemingly hopeless situation. Look up! Help is on the way. God may require you to give, out of your need. Simple obedience to his word will yield a fruitful harvest of blessings in your life.

Questions for Reflection

1. Have you ever been in a seemingly hopeless and helpless situation?
2. What did you do?
3. Did you cry out to God for help?
4. Did he send help?
5. What step of faith did God ask you to take?
6. Did you take the step?
7. How did you come out of the predicament?
8. Will you take a few minutes to thank God for bringing you out of that situation?
9. Will you share your testimony with a friend?

Meditation

I have been young, and now I'm old; yet have I not seen the righteous forsaken, nor his seed begging bread.

--Psalm 37:25

Memory Verse

Hear me, O Judah, and ye inhabitants of Jerusalem; Believe in the Lord your God, so shall ye be established; believe his prophets, so shall ye prosper.

--2 Chronicles 20:20b

Prayer

Dear Lord,

I bring every hopeless and helpless situation in my life and circumstance to you. I thank you, Lord that there is nothing that is impossible for you. I choose to trust you in the midst of the storm. I thank you for giving me victory in Jesus' name. Amen.

CHAPTER 15
THE PROPHET'S WIDOW

Now it came to pass, when the vessels were full,
that she said to her son, "Bring me another vessel."
And he said to her, "There is not another vessel."
So, the oil ceased. Then she came and told the man
of God. And he said, "Go, sell the oil and pay your
debt; and you and your sons live on the rest."

2 Kings 4:6-7

Elisha succeeded Elijah as the prophet of Israel. He became the principal of the school of prophets. Unfortunately, one of his students died, leaving behind a widow and two young sons. The widow told Elisha about her plight; her husband was indebted to some people, and the creditors were threatening to take her two sons as slaves.

Elisha asked her what she had in her house, she said there was nothing but a jar of oil. He told her to borrow as many vessels as she could and pour the oil in the bottles. She did that and had several bottles filled with the overflow from her last jar of oil. This was a miracle of multiplication. The prophet then told her to sell the oil, pay off the debt, and live off the rest. The impoverished woman became a business woman overnight! From the sale of her goods, she had enough money, not only to pay the debt, but also to keep for retirement. She was also able to keep and raise her sons. That is a beautiful story of full restoration.

God can deliver us from any kind of financial disaster. Sometimes the circumstances that lead to indebtedness are beyond our control. The great recession, loss of a job, under-employment, illness, and sudden bereavement could throw people into a pit of debt. No matter where you are, God wants to bring you out of the miry clay, and set your feet on the rock to stay. Cry out for help! He will lead you in the path of prosperity, and bless you again until you have more than enough.

Questions for Reflection

1. Are you or someone you know in debt?
2. Do you believe that God wants you to be debt-free?
3. What plans do you have to come out of debt?
4. Do you believe that God can set you free supernaturally?
5. What do you have left in your house? Cry out for wisdom. God can take what you have left, multiply it and restore your losses.

Meditation

The Lord will destroy the house of the proud, but he will establish the boundary of the widow.

--Proverbs 15:25

Memory Verse

I waited patiently for the Lord; and he inclined to me, and heard my cry. He also brought me up out of a horrible pit, out of the miry clay, and set my feet upon a rock, and established my steps. He has put a new song in my mouth - praise to our God; many will see it and fear, and will trust in the Lord.

--Psalm 40:1-3

Prayer

Lord Jesus,
   Thank you for sending this word of encouragement to me. I pray for divine wisdom and understanding in the management

of my finances. Show me the strategies that will make me a good steward of the resources you give to me. Bless me Lord, so that I can pay off my debts. Amen.

CHAPTER 16
THE SHUNAMITE WOMAN

*It came to pass, at the end of seven years, that the woman
returned from the land of the Philistines; and she went
to make an appeal to the king for her house and for her
land. So, the king appointed a certain officer for her,
saying, "Restore all that was hers, and all the proceeds of
the field from the day that she left the land until now."*

2 Kings 8:3,6b

The Shunamite woman was a wealthy lady in Israel who showed
kindness to Elisha the prophet. She was generous and hospi-
table. She made room for Elisha to stay in her house whenever he
was in her area. She was handsomely rewarded for her charitable
deeds. The Shunamite woman was barren. Elisha prayed for her to
have a child, and the Lord blessed her with a son. Then, the son
died of sunstroke, but the Shunamite woman stood her ground on
the promise of God. She called for Elisha the prophet who prayed
for the child and brought him back to life.

When Israel fell back into the sin of idolatry, God told Elisha that there would be a seven-year famine on the land. Elisha therefore advised the woman to go and live among the Philistines so that she would not have to participate in the recession. After seven years, the lady returned to Israel and went to the king to ask for her house and land. The Lord went ahead of her so she got to the palace at the time Elisha's servant was testifying to the king about the woman's son whose life was restored by Elisha's prayers.

The king was pleased with her; he ordered for all that should have come to her in the previous seven years to be restored to her in one day! I believe she was wealthier in her latter years than she was before the famine. If we are willing and obedient, we shall eat the good of the land. This woman was willing to be a blessing to God's servant. She was obedient to the instructions she was given. Despite the seven years of drought, the Lord preserved her lot and gave her full restoration. The Lord will restore everything the enemy stole from us, if we continue in the path of obedience. Amen.

Questions for Reflection

1. Do you think that the devil has stolen from you or someone you know?
2. Do you know anyone who is in a famine because they were swindled or scammed?
3. Have you ever experienced theft or robbery?
4. Do you believe that God can restore to you everything that was lost or stolen?
5. Will you share your story of a past loss with your pastor or mentor? Pray that the Lord will recover and restore all to you.

Meditation

If you are willing and obedient, you shall eat the good of the land.

--Isaiah1:19

Memory Verse

So, I will restore to you the years that the swarming locust has eaten, the crawling locust, the consuming locust, and the chewing locust, my great army which I sent among you.

--Joel 2:25

Prayer

Father God,
*   I thank you that you are the God of restoration. I thank you that you can restore all that the enemy stole from me, and more. I believe*

that I would see your goodness in the land of the living. Thank you for not only restoring my portion, but that of my descendants too. In Jesus' name, I pray. Amen.

CHAPTER 17
THE SIEGE OF SAMARIA

*Elisha replied, "The Lord says that by this time tomorrow
two gallons of flour or four gallons of barley grain
will be sold in the markets of Samaria for a dollar!"
And the people of Samaria rushed out and plundered
the camp of the Syrians. So, it was true that two
gallons of flour and four gallons of barley were sold
that day for one dollar, just as the Lord had said.*

2 Kings 7:1, 16b (TLB)

There was a famine in Samaria; in addition to that, the Syrian Army besieged the city, exacerbating the famine, and causing food to be very expensive. Things got so bad that people started eating their children (2 Kings 6:28-29)! When the word got to the king, he had a confrontation with the Elisha the prophet. Elisha then prophesied surplus and cheap food in 24 hours! The king's adviser thought it was impossible.

The Lord used the most unlikely weapons to defeat the enemy and restore food to the land. Some lepers decided to go to the camp of the Syrians. As the lepers approached the Syrian camp, the Lord made the Syrian army to hear the noise of chariots, and the noise of horses. They thought that the king of Israel had hired mightier kings against them, so they fled their camp leaving their food and goods behind.

The lepers ate their fill and went back to report the good news to the King of Israel. The king and the elders went to confirm their good fortune and truly, as the man of God had prophesied, food became available and affordable the following day. Unfortunately, the king's adviser who challenged the word of the Lord was trampled to death in the stampede for food. God is giving you a word of increase; do not listen to the voice of fear and doubt. In the most miraculous way and the most unusual circumstances, the Lord can stretch his hands to stop your famine in 24 hours. He will make the enemy pay back what he has stolen seven times! Amen.

Questions for Reflection

1. Has God given you a promise that looks impossible because of your present circumstance?
2. Is your situation strong enough to resist the word of God?
3. Just as we read in this devotional, God can bring a break-through in 24 hours. Do you see him doing the same thing for you?
4. Will you bring your situation of lack and desperation to God in prayer?
5. Will you praise him in advance for the answer?
6. Will you believe God for miracles? Look up, your redemption is nigh!

Meditation

Death and life are in the power of the tongue, and those who love it will eat its fruit.

--Proverbs 18:2

Memory Verse

Oh, that men would give thanks to the Lord for his goodness, and for his wonderful works to the children of men! For he satisfies the longing soul; and fills the hungry soul with goodness.

--Psalm 10:8-9

Prayer

Dear Lord,

I thank you for your power to deliver and to save. Speak a word over my life; speak a word of increase over my storehouses. Let your word turn my situation around for good. I praise you for the victory in Jesus' name. Amen.

PART IV

OVERFLOW, JESUS' STYLE

Jesus Christ is the express image of God the Father. Everything Jesus did while he was on earth was the will of his Father in heaven. Jesus performed a several miracles; he raised the dead, opened blind eyes, healed the lepers and the lame, stilled the storm, and set people free from demonic oppression. In addition to all these, he performed some very interesting miracles of provision. Jesus met the physical needs of the people; his very first miracle would occur at a wedding. He turned water into wine! The Lord will meet all our needs, great and small. He supplies our needs according to his riches in glory. In the next series of devotionals, we will see the several miracles of supply that graced the earthly ministry of our Lord and Savior, Jesus Christ.

CHAPTER 18

OVERFLOW OF WINE

When the master of the feast had tasted the water that was made wine, and did not know where it came from (but the servants who had drawn the water knew), the master of the feast called the bridegroom. And he said to him, "Every man at the beginning sets out the good wine, and when the guests have well drunk, then the inferior. You have kept the good wine until now!"

John 2:9-10

Jesus and his disciples were invited to a wedding at Cana of Galilee. This must have been a close relative's wedding, because Mary, his mom was there too. Somehow, they ran out of wine at the wedding. This was a situation that could lead to embarrassment at a wedding party. Jesus' mother asked him to help, but Jesus was hesitant. Mary knew Jesus could help, because she had probably experienced Jesus' intervention in such situations, while Jesus was growing up in her house. Instead of arguing with Jesus, she asked the servants to do whatsoever Jesus told them to do. That was the key to the miracle -- simple obedience.

Jesus asked the servants to fill the waterpots with water. They filled the pots to the brim. Then Jesus told them to draw some 'water' from the pot and take it to the governor of the feast. Somewhere on the way to the governor, the water had turned to wine! The wine tasted better than the original wine that ran out, so the governor thanked the bridegroom for reserving the best wine for last. I can imagine the great merriment that concluded that glorious wedding ceremony. This was Jesus' first miracle – abundant provision! If the first miracle was about abundance and overflow, then it confirms the fact that God delights in the prosperity of his people. Jesus performed this miracle to reiterate the fact that God always wants to bless his children.

Questions for Reflection

1. Have you ever been at a party where there was not food or drinks for the guests?
2. How did the host or hostess feel?
3. Was the situation rectified by someone bringing in the food later?
4. What was the mood at the party when more food was brought in?
5. How was the countenance of the host or hostess after all the guests had been fed?
6. What is the situation in your life right now that threatens to embarrass you?
7. Do you believe that Jesus can give you a solution for this situation?
8. Will you cry out to God to receive direction? Whatsoever he tells you to do, DO IT.

Meditation

He causes the grass to grow for the cattle, and vegetation for the service of man, that he may bring forth food from the earth, and wine that makes glad the heart of man, oil to make his face shine, and bread which strengthens man's heart.

--Psalms 104: 14-15

Memory Verse

And my God shall supply all your need according to his riches in glory by Christ Jesus.

--Philippians 4:19

Prayer

Lord,

I thank you that you that you promised to supply my needs according to your riches in glory, not according to my limitations. Therefore, Lord, I appropriate your riches for everything that I need for life and godliness, in Jesus' name. Amen.

CHAPTER 19

A GREAT CATCH OF FISH

*Simon said, "Master, we've been fishing hard all night
and haven't caught even a minnow. But if you say so, I'll
let out the nets." It was no sooner said than done—a huge
haul of fish, straining the nets' past capacity. They waved
to their partners in the other boat to come help them. They
filled both boats, nearly swamping them with the catch.*

Luke 5:5-7 MSG

Peter and his fishermen colleagues were done for the day. They
had tied up their boats and were already washing their nets.
They had had a fruitless day of labor and were about to go home
disappointed. The Jesus showed up! And their lives were changed
forever. Jesus had borrowed Peter's boat as a makeshift pulpit.

After the sermon, Jesus asked Peter to launch out into the
deep for a catch of fish. Peter explained to the Lord that the fish
were playing hide and seek, they hadn't caught one fish that day.
However, Peter chose to try again at the Jesus' command. He was

pleasantly surprised with a bumper harvest – OVERFLOW! They caught a net-breaking multitude of fishes. They had to call other fishermen to help carry the fish into the boat. Not only did their nets break, the boats were overloaded because of the weight of the fish! God had blessed them beyond their imagination!

Peter quickly recognized that Jesus was not just some broke preacher, who was looking for boats to borrow. There was something supernatural about him. Jesus was holy! Peter then realized his sinfulness because of this encounter he had with Jesus. He then asked Jesus to depart from him because he was afraid, but Jesus asked him and his friends not to be afraid but rather to come with him and be fishers of men.

Jesus can reveal himself to us in several ways. One of them is through miracles of abundance. If you are like Peter and his fishing friends, who had worked hard on a project without progress, admitted failure, and are now on the verge of quitting -- look again! A single encounter with Jesus will transform your mourning into dancing. He will turn it around!

Questions for Reflection

1. Can you recall a time you were working on a project and you were frustrated because you were not making headway?
2. What action did you take?
3. Did you quit and admit failure?
4. Did you pray about it to seek counsel of the Lord?
5. Did you depend on your own understanding?
6. After studying this chapter, would you do anything differently than you did the last time?
7. Do you believe that God can turn your situation around for good?

Meditation

Or do you despise the riches of his goodness, forbearance, and longsuffering, not knowing that the goodness of God leads you to repentance?

-- Romans 2:4

Memory Verse

Trust in the Lord with all your heart, and lean not on your own understanding; in all your ways acknowledge him, and he shall direct your paths.

--Proverbs 3: 5-6

Prayer

Lord,
I bring all my failed projects and unfinished ventures to you.
Speak your word of life into my situation. Open my eyes of under-
standing and show me the path of prosperity. Amen.

CHAPTER 20

ANOTHER GREAT CATCH OF FISH

Simon Peter said to them, "I am going fishing."
They said to him, "We are going with you also." They
went out and immediately got into the boat, and that
night they caught nothing. And he said to them, "Cast
the net on the right side of the boat, and you will find
some." So, they cast, and now they were not able to
draw it in because of the multitude of fish. The net
was full of large fish, one hundred and fifty-three; and
although there were so many, the net was not broken.

John 21:3,6,11

Jesus' disciples had been going everywhere with him for three years. After Jesus' death, their future looked bleak and blank. They did not know how to move forward. So, Peter decided to go back fishing. Five other disciples went fishing with him. They fished all night and caught nothing! That had happened before. The resurrected Christ appeared to them in the morning, he told them that they would find fish, if they cast their net to the right. They did so, and all the great fishes in the deep woke up and swam into their net. They recognized immediately that it was the Lord, because that was Jesus' *modus operandi* – transforming situations of lack to abundance.

Why would Jesus perform the miracle of the fish twice? He did this to remind the disciples that the call he placed on their lives the first time he performed this miracle was still valid. He had not changed his mind. He also did this to let them know that the time had come to fish for men. He gave them a visual image of the success that awaited them in bringing many souls to the kingdom. It is also noteworthy that the second time this miracle occurred, their fishing net remained intact, although the fish were large and many.

They had been trained for the previous three years, they were now ready to bear fruit that will last. Perhaps you made some mistake in the past in stewarding that which the Lord gave you. Maybe you lost some fortune through broken nets -- do not despair. The Lord will bless you again. He will give you a second chance. He will give you new ideas for increase, and give you stronger nets, so that you can retain the blessing. Amen.

Questions for Reflection

1. What advice would you give someone who is discouraged in ministry?
2. Are you that someone?
3. Why are you discouraged?
4. Did you experience failure?
5. Do you believe that God can still use you in this area of ministry?
6. Do you believe that he can use you in a greater way than he did the previous time?

Meditation

And let us not grow weary while doing good, for in due season we shall reap if we do not lose heart.

--Galatians 6:9

Memory Verse

Most assuredly, I say to you, he who believes in me, the works that I do he will do also; and greater works than these he will do, because I go to my father.

--John 14:12

Prayer

Dear Lord,

I thank you for your blessings on my life in the past. I thank you that the best is yet ahead of me. Make me a diligent and faithful steward of that which you have given me. Help me to maximize all the opportunities available to me. In Jesus' name. Amen.

CHAPTER 21
SANDWICHES IN THE DESERT

*Then he commanded the multitudes to sit down on
the grass. And he took the five loaves and the two
fish, and looking up to heaven, he blessed and broke
and gave the loaves to the disciples; and the disciples
gave to the multitudes. So, they all ate and were filled,
and they took up twelve baskets full of the fragments
that remained. Now those who had eaten were about
five thousand men, besides women and children.*

Mathew 14:19-21

Jesus had a day-long evangelical meeting in the desert. He
prayed for the people, healed the sick, and preached the gospel
of the kingdom. At the end of the day, the people were hungry.
Jesus told his disciples to give the people something to eat. They
explained to Jesus that the people were too many. They suggested
sending them home for dinner. Jesus used the occasion as an opportunity to teach his disciples that he could miraculously supply

physical needs also. He asked them how much food they had, they said only five loaves and two fish, and that was not enough to feed the multitude.

However, the Lord could see sandwiches in the making. He blessed the bread and fish and asked the disciples to distribute the food. Everybody at the crusade had their fill. There were 12 baskets of food left (overflow) after the miraculous dinner. If all the five thousand men had brought their wives, there would have been ten thousand people at the meeting. If all the wives had brought one child each, there would have been at least fifteen thousand people in attendance. This miracle transformed the community!

Questions for Reflection

1. Have you heard of, read about or been part of a community that was transformed by a miracle?
2. What was the miracle?
3. How did it happen?
4. How was the community different after the occasion?

Meditation

The eyes of all look expectantly to you, and you give them their food in due season. You open your hand, and satisfy the desire of every living thing.

--Psalm 145:15-16

Memory Verse

Blessed be God who daily loads us with benefits. The God of our salvation!

--Psalm 68:19

Prayer

Lord,

I pray for my community, my city, my state, and my nation. Let us experience your miracles of transformation that will bring many people to the kingdom in Jesus' name. Amen.

CHAPTER 22
SANDWICHES IN THE WILDERNESS

Now Jesus called His disciples to Himself and said, "I have compassion on the multitude, because they have now continued with me three days and have nothing to eat. And I do not want to send them away hungry, lest they faint on the way." So, they all ate and were filled, and they took up seven large baskets full of the fragments that were left. Now those who ate were four thousand men, besides women and children.

Matthew 15:32; 37-38

Jesus performed the miracle of multiplication of food twice. In the second instance, the people had been with him longer -- three days out in the wilderness. That was probably a retreat or a praying and fasting program, because Jesus said he would not send them away fasting. Again, the disciples wondered where they would find food to feed so many! They did not remember how they recently had sandwiches in the desert. Jesus again blessed the few loaves and fishes they had, the food multiplied and there were seven baskets of overflow!!!

Why did Jesus perform this miracle twice? He did that to reinforce the lesson in the minds of the disciples. Even after the second miracle, when Jesus talked about the leaven of the Pharisees, the disciples thought he was talking about shortage of bread. Then Jesus rebuked them that they should understand that shortage of bread is not an issue when he is on the scene (Mathew 16:6-12). We are needy people; we always need God's help. We might have experienced God's supernatural provision in the past. In our new season, we might encounter a similar challenge of lack or shortage. God wants you to know that if he helped you in times past, he will help you again. Have faith!

Questions for Reflection

1. What do you do when you encounter a difficult situation?
2. Do you take time to reflect on how God helped you in the past during a similar predicament?
3. Did that help you to overcome the problem with less anxiety?
4. Do you agree that thanking God for past victories gives you more confidence to handle your current battles?

Meditation

Bless the Lord, O my soul, and forget not all his benefits.

--Psalm 103:2

Memory Verse

And my God shall supply all your need according to his riches in glory by Christ Jesus.

-- Philippians 4:19

Prayer

Thank you Lord that you always meet my needs according to your riches in glory. Help me never to forget your goodness unto me. Let me continue to enjoy your loving kindness in the land of the living. Amen.

CHAPTER 23

ABUNDANT LIFE

The thief does not come except to steal, and to kill,
and to destroy. I have come that they may have life,
and that they may have it more abundantly.

John 10:10

J esus revealed his intention for our prosperity and wellbeing in
the verse above. Jesus and the father are one; just as we found
in Psalm 37 that God delights in the prosperity of his servants,
Jesus is also delighted when we prosper. Jesus desires for us to have
abundant life. He however warned us about the enemy, the thief,
the devil, who would like to steal, kill and destroy us, just as he did
in the Garden of Eden. Therefore, we must resist the devil, and
choose Life.

Jesus is the Way, the Truth, and the Life. He is the door of life
and the good shepherd. You can trust him with your life. He will
never leave you nor forsake you. He will not steal from you, kill, or
destroy you.

For I know the thoughts that I think toward you, says the Lord, thoughts of peace and not of evil, to give you a future and a hope.

--Jeremiah 29:11

For this purpose, was the Son of God manifested, that he might destroy the works of the devil.

--I John 3:8

Whatsoever the devil had been doing in our lives before we came to Christ will be destroyed by the power in the blood of Jesus. Everything the enemy stole from us shall be restored. The Lord will remove the evil beast from our land, and there shall be showers of blessing (Ezekiel 34:25-26).

Questions for Reflection

1. Have you or someone you know ever been robbed?
2. Were the thieves nice and pleasant?
3. Were they armed?
4. Did they steal valuables from you?
5. Were they apprehended?
6. Did you get your belongings back?
7. Has someone ever visited your home with an armload of gifts for you and your children?
8. Can you compare both situations?

Meditation

That if you confess with your mouth the Lord Jesus and believe in your heart that God has raised him from the dead, you will be saved.

--Romans 10:9

Memory Verse

For he says, "In an acceptable time I have heard you, and in the day of salvation I have helped you." Behold, now is the accepted time; behold, now is the day of salvation.

--2 Corinthians 6:2

Prayer

Lord Jesus,
I believe in my heart that you died for my sins, and that you rose on the third day for my justification. I confess my sins, and I ask for your forgiveness, save me Lord in your name. Amen.

PART V

OVERFLOW IN GIVING

Doxology

Praise God from whom all blessings flow;
Praise him all creatures here below;
Praise him above ye heavenly host;
Praise father, son and holy ghost.

Thomas Ken

God has extended his promise of overflow to us. What should be our response? We need to respond by accepting the blessings, and allowing our hearts to overflow with gratitude to God. We ought to be grateful to him in our hearts, and bless him with the fruit of our lips (Hebrews 13:15). When the blessings of God flow into our lives, we should not stop the flow with grumbling and murmuring, rather we should maintain the flow with a joyful heart of worship toward him. We also need to bless God back with our substance from the abundance that we have received. The next few devotionals will show us how to do just that.

CHAPTER 24

OVERFLOW IN WORSHIP

My heart is overflowing with a beautiful thought!
I will write a lovely poem to the King, for I am as
full of words as the speediest writer pouring.

Psalm 45:1 (TLB)

G iving to God starts with a heart of worship; God loves a cheerful giver. God made it clear to the children of Israel that he had no use for all their cattle and animal offerings, if they would not praise him from their hearts (Psalm 50:9-10). God requires our hearts before our substance. He requires our obedience and love. He wants us to worship him with our money and material gifts because we love and appreciate him, and not begrudgingly or out of necessity (2 Cor. 9:7).

Psalm 45 is a beautiful rendition of the expression of praise, overflowing from the heart of a true worshiper. In the verse above, the psalmist describes how those words are flowing from the depths of his heart. He had been meditating on God's goodness and mercy on his life. David thought about the Lord's greatness and might, he pondered on God's good attributes. He hid those words in his heart until he could no longer contain them. The psalmist had to write the words so others could read his thoughts.

This is how we ought to love and worship the Lord; studying the word, meditating on it, and continually reminiscing about the goodness of God in our lives. This would keep our hearts tender and grateful; we would be able to praise God from a deep fountain of thankfulness. When we praise and worship God from our hearts, the heavens open upon us, and God's blessings flow into our lives.

Questions for Reflection

1. Do you enjoy worshipping God?
2. What is your favorite way of expressing your worship?
3. What types of congregational worship inspire you most?
4. Do you have testimonies of God's specific response to your worship at a season in your life?
5. How can you improve your personal worship time before the Lord?

Meditation

Praise the Lord!
Praise God in His sanctuary;
Praise Him in His mighty firmament!
Praise Him for His mighty acts;
Praise Him according to His excellent greatness!
Praise Him with the sound of the trumpet;
Praise Him with the lute and harp!
Praise Him with the timbrel and dance;
Praise Him with stringed instruments and flutes!
Praise Him with loud cymbals;
Praise Him with clashing cymbals!
Let everything that has breath praise the Lord.
Praise the Lord!

--Psalm 150

Memory Verse

It is good to give thanks to the Lord, and to sing praises to your name, O most high;

To declare your lovingkindness in the morning, and your faithfulness every night.

--Psalm 92:1-2

Prayer

Dear Lord Jesus,

I love you. Teach my heart to hunger and thirst after you. Teach my spirit to worship you in spirit and in truth. Cleanse me and sanctify me. Let pure unadulterated praise flow from life to your throne. Let my praises rise up to you with a sweet -smelling savor. Let my worship be acceptable in your sight. Amen.

CHAPTER 25
ESTABLISH THE GIVING CYCLE

*"Give, and it will be given to you, a good measure—pressed down, shaken, **overflowing**—they will pour out into your lap. For with the measure by which you measure out, it will be measured out to you in return".*

Luke 6:38 (LEB)

When we give to God, he gives back to us. Jesus was teaching that we should not judge others, lest we be judged. He used the concept of giving as an example to illustrate the cycle of getting back what we send out. He went further to explain that when we give to God, he will give back to us through other people. What we will receive as a reward for our seed sown, will be exponentially greater than what we gave.

The gift sown is multiplied, and you can reap several folds of whatever was sown. The same measure that you mete to others, shall be measured back to you. The measure is not necessarily the amount you gave, it is the proportion of your gift compared to the whole. The more we give of our substance, the more we will receive manifold blessings. Just as we established the flow of worship, the Lord expects us to establish a cycle of giving to him regularly and cheerfully.

> *But this I say: He who sows sparingly will also reap sparingly, and he who sows bountifully will also reap bountifully. So, let each one give as he purposes in his heart, not grudgingly or of necessity; for God loves a cheerful giver*

> (2 Corinthians 9:6-7).

Questions for Reflection

1. Do you believe that everything you have is a gift from God?
2. Would you give a portion back to God from what you received from him?
3. Do you believe in the law of sowing and reaping?
4. Can you recall a time that you gave to God and were rewarded abundantly by people giving back to you?
5. Have you ever thought that giving back to God is not necessary?
6. Do you think that giving back to God is unscriptural?

Meditation

Every good gift and every perfect gift is from above, and comes down from the father of lights, with whom there is no variation or shadow of turning.

--James 1:17

Memory Verse

On the first day of the week let each one of you lay something aside, storing up as he may prosper, that there be no collections when I come.

--1 Corinthians 16:2

Prayer

Dear Lord,
I praise you for all your blessings that are flowing into my life. I receive the grace of giving so I can give back to you cheerfully and regularly. Thank you for your promise to increase me on every side. Amen.

CHAPTER 26

GIVE GOD THE FIRST AND THE BEST

*Honor God with everything you own; give
him the **first and the best**. Your barns will
burst, your wine vats will brim over*

Proverbs 3:9-10 (MSG)

As followers of Jesus Christ and the redeemed of the Lord, we need to honor the Lord with our substance. Jesus said that you cannot serve God and mammon. (Mathew 6:24b). You must choose one. If we believe that all our blessings flow from God, then we should honor him with our finances. Giving back to God from that which he has given to us should be our lifestyle. The bible makes it clear how God wants us to give. He wants us to give him the first fruits. In modern language that will be the first part of our income. The Israelites gave God the first of their harvest.

They did not eat out of the harvest until they had given the first part to God.

When we give God the first, he blesses the rest. We should be careful not to give to God last, or later. It is important that our spending pattern reflects our commitment and allegiance to God. Giving to God first should be the Christian's priority. Giving God the first breaks every agreement with the spirit of mammon. When we give God first, we are telling God that we are grateful for his provision; and we let the enemy know that we will not bow down to mammon.

The promise from the verse above is that when we give God the first of our fruits, he will respond to us with an overflow of blessings. In modern language, that will be overflowing bank accounts with enough for our needs, and a lot leftover for our wants (wine). God also wants the best, and rightfully so, because he is worthy. In the Old Testament, the Israelites worshipped the Lord with animal sacrifices. They were not allowed to give sick or maimed animals as offerings. The bull or lamb used for the sacrifice must be without blemish (Numbers 29:8).

Questions for Reflection

1. Do you get irritated or do you rejoice when you get the opportunity to give to God?
2. Do you consider yourself a cheerful giver?
3. Do you give to God first?
4. Do you give God the best?
5. If you answered "NO" to one or more questions (2-4), then you need to change your attitude towards giving.
6. After reading the devotional for today, do you realize the need for change?
7. Are you willing and ready to make the necessary changes?

Meditation

No servant can serve two masters; for either he will hate the one and love the other, or else he will be loyal to the one and despise the other. You cannot serve God and mammon.

--Luke 16:13

Memory Verse

Moreover, it is required in stewards that one be found faithful.

--1 Corinthians 4:2

Prayer

Father Lord,
    I receive the grace to acknowledge you first in my finances. I repent for all the times that I have put you later or last. Forgive me and help me to be a faithful steward of your blessings on my life. I love you Lord. I will not yield to the dictates of mammon. Amen.

CHAPTER 27
TITHES AND OFFERINGS

*Then Melchizedek king of Salem brought out bread
and wine; he was the priest of God most high. And
he blessed him and said: "Blessed be Abram of God
most high, possessor of heaven and earth; and blessed
be God most high, who has delivered your enemies
into your hand." And he gave him a tithe of all.*

Genesis 14:18-20

A braham won the battle against Chedorlaomer (Genesis 14:14-
16), and he got a lot of plunder. On his way back from the war,
he met Melchizedek who was a priest of God. Abraham gave the
tithes of all to him. Similarly, Jacob made a deal with God on his
way to Laban's house, when God appeared to him. He promised to
give God a tithe of all his income, if God gave him a successful journey (Gen: 28:22). God did, and Jacob obviously fulfilled his vows.

Giving of the tithe would later become a statute for the children of Israel. The Israelites were required to give ten (10) percent

of their income to God. We, as New Testament Christians also should continue in tithing because we have been grafted into the Abrahamic covenant. The Levites were the priesthood tribe of the Israelites. They were not required to do secular work; their job was to minister to the Lord in the tabernacle or temple. They were to receive the tithes from the Israelites. The tithes of the people served as remuneration for the priests.

The Israelites also gave several types of offerings in addition to the tithe as was required by the law of Moses. There were grain offerings, peace offerings, sin offerings, first fruits and other offerings for special occasions (Leviticus 1-7). God gave the children of Israel several opportunities to give, so that they would have numerous opportunities to be blessed in return. We also have the same advantage. Let us worship the Lord with our tithes and offerings.

Questions for Reflection

1. Do you believe in tithing?
2. If not, why?
3. If yes, have you been faithful to give your tithes and offerings?
4. Do you have a testimony of a positive change in your finances when you started tithing diligently?
5. Do you recall a time that you were not tithing?
6. What was your experience in your finances at that time?
7. Were you blessed more as a tither than as a non-tither?

Meditation

Here mortal men receive tithes, but there he receives them, of whom it is witnessed that he lives.

--Hebrews 7:8

Memory Verse

Bring all the tithes into the storehouse, that there may be food in my house, and try me now in this," says the Lord of hosts, "If I will not open for you the windows of heaven and pour out for you such blessing that there will not be room enough to receive it.

--Malachi 3:10

Prayer

Dear Lord,

I want to obey you in all things. I ask for forgiveness for not paying my tithes faithfully and on time. Open my eyes of understanding. Let me be a cheerful giver. I want to worship you with all I have. Amen.

CHAPTER 28
GIVE AT EVERY OPPORTUNITY

Cast your bread upon the waters, for you will find
it after many days. Give a serving to seven, and
also to eight, for you do not know what evil will
be on the earth. In the morning sow your seed,
and in the evening, do not withhold your hand;
for you do not know which will prosper, either this
or that, or whether both alike will be good.

Ecclesiastes 11:1-2, 6 (KJV).

The bible encourages us to give as often as we can. In addition to giving our tithes and offerings to our local church, we are to give to other causes that God might lay on our hearts. Everything we have belongs to God, we should therefore steward whatsoever we have received with godly fear. Giving several times and in several places, ensures our harvest, and increases our chances of reaping multiple times. Some seeds grow and bring harvest fast, other seeds take some time; while we are waiting for the big seed to germinate, we eat from the harvest of the smaller seeds we have sown.

Also, some small seeds yield huge harvests especially if the seed was precious. God works in mysterious ways; he gives seed to the sower and bread to the eater (Isaiah 55:10). When he gives us seed, and we sow it faithfully, we are rewarded with bread to eat, and more seeds to plant. The more opportunities we take to give, the higher our chances of reaping a bumper harvest.

Now may he who supplies seed to the sower, and bread for food, supply and multiply the seed you have sown and increase the fruits of your righteousness.

--2 Corinthians 9:10

Questions for Reflection

1. As discussed in this devotional, sowing is when we give of our money (or other resources to God), and reaping is when we experience a manifestation of rewards for the gift we gave. Have you experienced God at this level?
2. Did you sow a gift, or give tithe or offering? Were you blessed with tangible financial increase?
3. When you had an unexpected raise at work, or a new job, were you able to quickly link this blessing to a sacrificial seed you planted in the kingdom?
4. When you give, do you expect God to bless you in return?
5. Do you know that manifold blessings coming into our lives because of our giving, is God's promise to us?
6. Have you sown a large, or very precious seed? Are you still awaiting the harvest? If yes, be patient. Your harvest will come in due season.

Meditation

While the earth remains, seedtime and harvest, cold and heat, winter and summer, and day and night shall not cease.

--Genesis 8:22

Memory Verse

And let us not grow weary while doing good, for in due season we shall reap if we do not lose heart.

--Galatians 6:9

Prayer

Lord Jesus,

Help me to recognize and maximize the opportunities you have for me to sow into the kingdom. Give me the patience to wait for my harvest. Open my eyes to see and remove anything in my life that might block or delay my harvest. Amen.

PART VI
HINDRANCES TO OVERFLOW

The next series of devotionals are a very important part of this book. Since God has given us the great promises of his blessings and overflow, he has also warned us of the consequences of not obeying his word. If you have noticed constant lack and shortage in your finances, you need to ask yourself some questions (2 Corinthians 13:5). "Am I doing something wrong?" Another question you might want to ask is, "Have I neglected something I should be doing?" The children of Israel in their walk with God had several episodes of disobeying God. And every time that happened, they could not experience God's overflowing blessings. We do not want to repeat that cycle. In the next few chapters we will examine the hindrances to overflow, so that we can avoid the pitfalls.

CHAPTER 29

DISOBEDIENCE TO GOD

*Because you did not serve the Lord your God with
joy and gladness of heart, for the abundance of
everything, therefore you shall serve your enemies,
whom the Lord will send against you, in hunger, in
thirst, in nakedness, and in need of everything.*

Deuteronomy 28:47-48b

The promise of the blessing given to the nation of Israel in Deuteronomy 28 is conditional. The only condition attached was obedience to God's commandments. However, in the same chapter, the bible warned of the grave consequences of living in disobedience to God's laws. God wants us to serve him and obey him with gladness and joy. He does not want us to worship him out of necessity or compulsion. He desires true worship from our grateful hearts. If we do this, we will be blessed with the abundance of all things. On the other hand, God told the Israelites, that if they would not serve him gladly, they would serve their enemies, who would put them in a perpetual state of lack.

We see examples of this in the history of the Israelites; anytime they did not serve God faithfully, their enemies prevailed over them. May God have mercy on us, and may we never serve our enemies. If we continue to experience lack and poverty in our lives, we need to ask the Lord to reveal to us any area of our lives that may be in alignment with the enemy. Alignment with the enemy could be willful sin in our lives, or idolatry, whereby we worship a false god. We should break all such alignments once they are revealed. If we continue to serve and worship the Lord gladly, the tide will turn and we will experience continuous and uninterrupted abundance in all things. Amen.

Questions for Reflection

1. The only condition for the blessings of Deuteronomy 28 is obedience to God. Would you be willing to obey God to receive his blessings?
2. Is it fair for us to worship other gods and expect God to keep blessing us?
3. Are idols true gods?
4. Do idols bless their worshippers?
5. Why do people worship idols?
6. After God has delivered us from the bondage of sin and idol worship, what should be our response to him?
7. Are you a happy disciple of Jesus Christ?

Meditation

Serve the Lord with gladness; come before his presence with singing.

--Psalm 100:2

Memory Verse

If they obey and serve him, they shall spend their days in prosperity, and their years in pleasures.

--Job 36:11

Prayer

Lord Jesus,
Thank you for saving me. Lord, save me to the uttermost. Deliver me from presumptuous sins and the consequences of idolatry. Open

my eyes of understanding. Help me not to submit to the enemy in my mind, thoughts, or actions. Heal me Lord, and I will be healed. Amen.

CHAPTER 30
IDOLATRY

You shall not make for yourself a carved image—
any likeness of anything that is in heaven above, or
that is in the earth beneath, or that is in the water
under the earth; you shall not bow down to them nor
serve them. For I, the Lord your God, am a jealous
God, visiting the iniquity of the fathers upon the
children to the third and fourth generations of those
who hate me, but showing mercy to thousands, to
those who love me and keep my commandments.

Exodus 20:4-6

I dolatry is the most grievous sin in God's sight. God warned the nation of Israel expressly against this sin. The consequences for idol worship are immense and terrible. This was the very first commandment, that Israel would not worship idols. It was also the first rebellion of the nation. The Israelites worshipped the golden calf in the wilderness, and for that reason, that generation did not inherit the promised land. They all perished on the way.

Moses warned the Israelites again, in Deuteronomy 28, as they prepared to enter the land of Canaan, that if they fell again into idolatry, the results would be disastrous and catastrophic. Unfortunately, the nation of Israel did not always serve God. They allowed themselves to be seduced into worshipping the idols of Canaan. Therefore, the Lord was angry with them and he allowed them to go into captivity.

May we never go into captivity. Amen. Should we discover that there is generational poverty, shortage and lack in our lineage, it could be because our ancestors had worshipped idols. We need to repent of generational idolatry and ask for God to deliver us from all the negative results of idol worship in our bloodline. We also need to continue to worship God with a single mind and focus. If we refuse to worship any god that is not Yahweh, the curses will be removed and prosperity will be restored back to us and our children in Jesus' name. Amen.

Questions for Reflection

1. What is a generation?
2. What is a lineage or bloodline?
3. What is generational idolatry?
4. How did idolatry become a generational sin for the Israelites?
5. Was God happy with them for their idolatry?
6. What was the consequence of their idol worship?
7. Have you worshipped idols in the past?
8. Do you know of idolatry in any of your ancestors? Repent of idolatry and pray that God will cleanse your bloodline from the effects of idol worship.

Meditation

*Who may ascend into the hill of the Lord? Or who may stand in His holy place? He who has clean hands and a pure heart, who **has not lifted up his soul to an idol**, nor sworn deceitfully. He shall receive blessing from the Lord, and righteousness from the God of his salvation.*

--Psalm 24: 3-5

Memory Verse

And if it seems evil to you to serve the Lord, choose for yourselves this day whom you will serve, whether the gods which your fathers served that were on the other side of the river, or the gods of the Amorites, in whose land you dwell. But as for me and my house, we will serve the Lord.

--Joshua 24:15

Prayer

Dear Lord,

I thank you for your blood that was shed for me on Calvary. Let your blood do a thorough cleansing of my bloodline. Deliver me and my children from the effects of idol worship. Create in me a clean heart. Renew a right spirit within me. Amen.

CHAPTER 31
FAILURE TO SOW

He who observes the wind will not sow, and
he who regards the clouds will not reap.

Ecclesiastes 11:4 KJV

Another major hindrance to overflow is not giving at all. There are principles of giving that we must observe, if we want to experience continuous overflow in our finances. The bible says that;

While the earth remains, seedtime and harvest, cold and heat, win-
ter and summer, and day and night shall not cease.

--Genesis 8:32;

Give and it will be given to you: good measure, pressed down, shaken together, and running over will be put into your bosom. For with the same measure that you use, it will be measured back to you.

-- Luke 6:38

If there are no seeds sown, there should be no expectation of any harvest. If we do not give, we should not expect to receive. In the verse above (Ecclesiastes 11:4), the preacher warns about being too careful, and not wanting to take risks. When the Holy Spirit asks you to give, do you obey promptly? Do you look at your bank account and 'see every reason why it is not the right time to sow'? Do you immediately start thinking of other things you could use the money for?

The Holy Spirit nudged a woman in the bible to pour out her expensive perfume on Jesus. She obeyed. However, some people in the room were not happy that she had lavished such an expensive gift on the Lord. They immediately thought of something else to do with the perfume -- sell it and give the money to the poor.

Jesus rebuked them for their myopic views (Mark 14:3-8). This lady had received her dead alive; she was Lazarus' sister. She poured out her expensive perfume in overflowing gratitude to the Lord for the great deliverance that was wrought in her life. By anointing the Lord's body at that time, she prepared his body for his death and burial. When we give diligently to the Lord, whether it is convenient or not, when we sow without looking at the winds, we position ourselves for unprecedented returns of blessings.

Questions for Reflection

1. Do you consider yourself a generous giver?
2. Do you obey quickly and gladly when the Holy Spirit prompts you to give above your tithe?
3. Do you give outside of your comfort zone, that is when it is not convenient?
4. What was the result of your sacrificial giving?

Share your testimony with a friend.

Meditation

Those who sow in tears shall reap in joy. He who continually goes forth weeping, bearing seed for sowing, shall doubtless come again with rejoicing, bringing his sheaves with him.

--Psalm 126: 5-6

Memory Verse

The generous soul will be made rich, and he who waters will also be watered himself.

--Proverbs 11:25

Prayer

Dear Lord,
      Bless me and make me a blessing as you promised. Deliver me from the spirit of greed, and stinginess. Give me freedom in my spirit and willingness to be a channel for your supplies to flow into the kingdom. Use me for your glory. Amen.

CHAPTER 32
NEGLECTING GOD'S HOUSE

*Why is everyone saying it is not the right time for
rebuilding my temple?" asks the Lord. His reply to
them is this: "Is it then the right time for you to live in
luxurious homes, when the temple lies in ruins? Look
at the result: You plant much but harvest little. You
have scarcely enough to eat or drink and not enough
clothes to keep you warm. Your income disappears, as
though you were putting it into pockets filled with holes!*

Haggai 1:2-6 (TLB)

There is an interesting little story tucked away in a two-chapter
book in the bible-the book of Haggai. The Israelites were just
returning from the Babylonian captivity and were so busy rebuilding their homes that they forgot to rebuild the temple of the Lord.
They imagined that they could do that at a convenient time.

However, God had a totally different idea. He told them through
the prophet Haggai that their lack of interest in rebuilding his

house was the reason for all their economic woes. He also promised to bless them if they would rebuild the temple. Thankfully, this time the Israelites quickly repented and proceeded to start rebuilding the house of the Lord. The Lord pronounced a blessing on them and turned their famine into plenty.

As followers of Jesus Christ, many of us belong to a local church. God expects us to be financial members of the body of Christ to which he has appointed us. From time to time, when there is a need for the place of meeting, we may be called upon to give special offerings to meet the need. This special offering may be sacrificial for us. But the Lord will give us special blessings for sowing at such times.

Seek first the kingdom of God and his righteousness, and all these things shall be added to you

(Mathew 6:33).

Questions for Reflection

1. Do you give your tithes to the local church to which you belong?
2. Have you participated in any church building fund (which may require you to go above your tithe)?
3. Do you believe that the smooth running of your local church should be financed by the parishioners?
4. If given the opportunity, will you encourage other members of your local church to give to the church?
5. Can you recall a specific blessing that was linked to a building project offering that you gave?

Record your testimony in a journal.

Meditation

And I told them of the hand of my God which had been good upon me, and also of the king's words that he had spoken to me. So, they said, "Let us rise up and build." Then they set their hands to this good work.

--Nehemiah 2:18

Memory Verse

Then at the king's command they made a chest, and set it outside at the gate of the house of the LORD. Thus they did day by day, and gathered money in abundance.

–2 Chronicles 24:8 &10

Prayer

Father Lord,
    Make me a builder and a rebuilder. Empower me to be a blessing to your household. Let me never be found wanting when duty calls. Amen.

CHAPTER 33

WITHHOLDING THE BEST

"Yet you say, 'When did we ever despise your name?'
When you offer polluted sacrifices on my altar.
'Polluted sacrifices? When have we ever done a
thing like that?' Every time you say, 'Don't bother
bringing anything very valuable to offer to God!'"

Malachi 1: 6-7 (TLB)

G od will not accept defiled offerings on his altar. In the scriptures above, the Lord God accused the priests of offering blemished animals to him. The law of Moses made it clear that God wanted the best of the animals in the flock as sacrifice, and warned against offering sick and blind animals on his altar.

You shall present a burnt offering to the Lord as a sweet aroma: one young bull, one ram, and seven lambs in their first year. Be sure they are without blemish.

--Numbers 29:8

At that time in the history of the Israelites, the people were doing the exact opposite. They brought just any animal they could find-even stolen ones! for offering. The priests, who should have known better, did not correct them. So, God was angry with the priests for allowing the people to offer to him less than perfect animals. Therefore, he rejected their offerings.

God also spoke specifically of people who, when they were in trouble, vowed to give their best if God delivered them. As soon as God bailed them out of the trouble, they paid their vows with maimed animals while keeping the healthy ones back. God said that was disrespectful, and anyone who did that would be under a curse from God.

This is a major hindrance to overflow; sometimes we vow before God to give a certain amount, when he answers our prayers. And then we change our minds and give some paltry sum after we might have received the miracle. Such attitude will truncate the overflow that God is sending into our lives. We must give God the best that we promised; because he deserves it for all his goodness and mercy over our lives.

Questions for Reflection

1. If you were going to visit the governor of your state, and you had to take a gift, would you give him a broken non-consequential gift, wrapped with ordinary paper?
2. Would you find the best gift you could afford, and wrap it with bows and ribbons?
3. How would the governor respond when he opens the broken gift?
4. How would he respond on opening the exquisite gift?
5. Who would he invite back to the state house, the guest with the thoughtful gift or the guest with the damaged gift?
6. If we respect our earthly leaders and dignitaries, should we not honor God, our father with the best of what we have? May God help us. Amen.

Meditation

For I, the Lord, love justice; I hate robbery for burnt offering; I will direct their work in truth, and will make with them an everlasting covenant.

--Isaiah 61:8

Memory Verse

You shall not sacrifice to the Lord your God a bull or sheep which has any blemish or defect, for that is an abomination to the Lord your God.

--Deuteronomy 17:1

Prayer

Father Lord,

   You are merciful and gracious. You do not deal with me accord-
ing to my iniquities. Forgive me for all the times I have not rever-
enced you in my giving. Lord, help me to be diligent in giving my
best to you always. I praise you Lord because you are worthy. Amen.

CHAPTER 34

STEALING FROM GOD

"Will a man rob God? Yet you have robbed me! But you say, 'In what way have we robbed you?' In tithes and offerings. You are cursed with a curse, for you have robbed me, even this whole nation. Bring all the tithes into the storehouse, that there may be food in my house, and try me now in this," says the LORD of hosts, "if I will not open for you the windows of heaven, and pour out for you such blessing that there will not be room enough to receive it. And I will rebuke the devourer for your sakes, so that he will not destroy the fruit of your ground, nor shall the vine fail to bear fruit for you in the field," says the LORD of hosts; "and all nations will call you blessed, for you will be a delightful land," says the LORD of hosts.

Malachi 3: 8-12

G od continued his discourse on giving, with the children of Israel through prophet Malachi. He accused the whole nation of stealing from him. They quickly denied, saying that it is not feasible for men to steal from God. Then God graciously showed them their sin of omission, they had not been giving their tithes and offerings, which was the reason for the economic recession in the nation at that time. God struck a deal with them. He asked them to put him to test by giving their full tithes, and offerings as commanded by the law of Moses.

The Lord gave specific promises of abundant economic blessings on those who would give their tithes:

(a) The windows of heaven will open.
(b) Blessings will be released through the open windows.
(c) More storehouses will be built to accommodate the blessings.
(d) The devourer will be rebuked.
(e) There will be no premature loss of crops.

If we are not giving the whole tithe and offerings as and when due (Proverbs 11:24), we may find ourselves in a financial mess. But if we return to God and put him to test with our tithes, there will be a divine reversal of bad fortune. Everything that was stolen shall be restored and we will be restored to the undue overflow that God planned for our lives.

Questions for Reflection

1. Do you believe that paying your tithe can save you from financial distress?
2. Have you ever put God to test about your tithes and offering?
3. Did God "pass the test"? Did God come through for you?
4. Have you continued to tithe since then?
5. If not, why?

If you have not been tithing, this is your opportunity to put God to test. Pay your tithe and watch God bless you back. Paying your tithes and offerings brings divine insurance on your money. The enemy will have no access to your source of income.

Meditation

There you shall take your burnt offerings, your sacrifices, your tithes, the heave offerings of your hand, your vowed offerings, your freewill offerings, and the firstborn of your herds and flocks.

--Deuteronomy 12:6

Memory Verse

But he whose genealogy is not derived from them received tithes from Abraham and blessed him who had the promises.

--Hebrews 7:6

Prayer

Dear Lord,

Thank you for opening my eyes of understanding. Forgive me for all the times I did not give my tithes and offerings. Help me to be faithful. Break every curse on my income by the power in your blood. In Jesus' name. Amen.

PART VII
MORE HINDRANCES TO OVERFLOW

I would like to dig further into the issues that might be hindering the blessings of God in our lives. While the last few devotionals discussed our negative giving habits, the next ones will be about our attitude towards God.

The bible says that God is a rewarder of them that seek him and everyone who comes to God must believe that he is (Hebrews 11:6). God has given us all these great promises, but some people will not experience the overflow due to unbelief, and general lack of respect for the voice of God (Psalm 29). This is another area where the enemy may be robbing us of our inheritance. May our inner eyes be opened as we examine the next series of devotionals. Amen.

CHAPTER 35

NEGATIVE TALK

*And all the children of Israel complained against
Moses and Aaron, and the whole congregation said
to them, "If only we had died in the land of Egypt!
Or if only we had died in this wilderness! Why has
the Lord brought us to this land to fall by the sword,
that our wives and children should become victims?
Would it not be better for us to return to Egypt?"
"Say to them, "'As I live,' says the Lord, 'just as you
have spoken in my hearing, so I will do to you.'"*

Numbers 14:2-3,28

G od promised Abraham that he would give the land of Canaan,
a land that flowed with milk and honey to his descendants.
God fulfilled this promise 400 years later, when Moses delivered
the children of Israel out of slavery so that they could proceed to
possess the promise. Moses sent 12 spies, one from each tribe to
assess the land. The spies came back with a negative report. True,

the land was flowing with milk and honey with huge magnificent grapes, but there were giants in the land. The spies thought that going in to possess the land was a bad idea; after all, they would probably lose their lives in the process.

Their negative report spurred a rebellious spree in which the children of Israel murmured against the Lord. Joshua and Caleb, however, had a positive report; they encouraged the people, saying that God would give them the land despite the giants. The people would hear none of it; they were more comfortable going with report from the negative doom and gloom majority. God responded to them by giving them exactly what they spoke in his ears. The ten spies that brought the negative report died before the Lord.

The whole generation of murmurers perished in the wilderness as they wandered around for forty years, in fulfillment of the negative prophecy they spoke against themselves. Joshua and Caleb went on to lead the younger generation into the land of Canaan, because they believed God, and their speech was different. We also have the promise of the overflow, and we need to confess the promise. We need to speak blessings over our lives, our homes and our children. We need to speak into our atmosphere what we want God to hear in his ears. We need to declare boldly what we want his angels to perform on our behalf. When we declare the promises of the Lord with faith in our hearts, we will experience the fullness of his promises just like Joshua and Caleb.

Questions for Reflection

1. What should be our attitude as Christians when we go through trials?
2. Are trials an excuse for us to speak negatively about our circumstance?
3. Are you going through a financial difficulty right now?
4. How are you responding to the pressure?
5. Are you speaking negativity into your atmosphere or are you speaking faith?
6. If you think you have no faith, take some time to study and listen to the word of God. Faith comes by hearing and hearing by the word of God (Romans 10:17).
7. Start declaring God's promises over your finances.

Meditation

Death and life are in the power of the tongue, and those who love it will eat its fruit.

--Proverbs 18:21

Memory Verse

While it is said: "Today, if you will hear his voice, do not harden your hearts as in the rebellion."

--Hebrews 3:15

Prayer

Dear Lord,
Forgive me for every negative word that I have spoken concerning my finances. I pray, Lord, that your blood will neutralize the

effects of negative words that were spoken against me, or that I spoke against myself. Let every negative cycle that was set in place by those words be broken and discontinued. Let your own good thoughts concerning me begin to come to manifestation. Amen.

CHAPTER 36
LIMITING GOD

Yes, they spoke against God: they said, "Can God prepare a table in the wilderness? Behold, he struck the rock, so that the waters gushed out, and the streams overflowed. Can he give bread also? Can he provide meat for his people?" Yes, again and again they tempted God, and limited the Holy One of Israel.

Psalm 78:19-20, 41

When God brought the children of Israel out of the nation of Egypt, he did so with a strong and outstretched arm. He brought Egypt to its knees to set Israel free from 400 years of slavery. He did terrible and mighty things such as afflicting the Egyptians with the ten plagues. God also parted the Red Sea so that the children of Israel could escape Pharaoh's army.

Furthermore, when they crossed over into the wilderness, they experienced supernatural supplies. God gave them water from the rock and manna from heaven. Despite all these miracles, the

Israelites were not impressed. They grumbled and complained in their hearts. They were asking if God could give them meat, so that they could have a full course meal in the wilderness.

God was angry with them, he gave them the desires of their hearts, but he sent leanness to their souls. He sent quail into the midst of the camp and while the meat was yet in their teeth, some of them fell dead; ruining the dinner for the whole assembly!

Be careful for nothing but by prayer and thanksgiving, let your requests be made known to God, and my God shall supply your needs according to his riches in glory.

--Philippians 4:19

The children of Israel should have asked God politely and in faith, when they were craving for meat. Their attitude showed that they did not believe that God could meet their need, although they had experienced many miracles. God was obviously not happy with their unbelief. Are you in an economic wilderness? Don't look at your circumstance; rather consider the wonderful things that God had done in your life before. Even in famine, God can open unexpected sources of provision. Ask in faith with prayers and thanksgiving. Then, thank God in anticipation of the answer to your prayers.

Questions for Reflection

1. Can you recall the wonderful things that God did in your own life?
2. Can you also recall when God did something wonderful in the life of someone close to you?
3. Do you remember reading or listening to somebody's testimony of God's goodness?
4. Do you remember specifically a major financial miracle God wrought in your life?
5. Do you know of someone close or distant to you who received a massive financial breakthrough from God?
6. Are you going through the valley of the shadow of fiscal crisis?
7. Are you in the "valley of the shadow of debt"? The valley of the shadow of debt is the valley of the shadow of financial death. But on the other side is the banquet table and overflowing anointing for increase.
8. Will you trust God to lead you out of the valley and get you to the other side?
9. Do you remember the former miracles you had and the ones you heard about?

Encourage yourself in the Lord. You will testify of the goodness of the Lord in the land of the living.

Meditation

I will lift up my eyes to the hills—
From whence comes my help?
My help comes from the LORD,
Who made heaven and earth.
He will not allow your foot to be moved;

He who keeps you will not slumber.
Behold, he who keeps Israel
Shall neither slumber nor sleep.
The LORD is your keeper;
The LORD is your shade at your right hand.
The sun shall not strike you by day,
Nor the moon by night.
The LORD shall preserve you from all evil;
He shall preserve your soul.
The LORD shall preserve your going out and your coming in
From this time forth, and even forevermore.

--Psalm 121

Memory Verse

I will lift up my eyes to the hills—
From whence comes my help?
My help comes from the LORD,
Who made heaven and earth.

--Psalm 121: 1-2

Prayer

Father God,
I repent of limiting you in my imagination. I repent of not trusting you fully when I cannot see where my supply is coming from. Help me to recall your good hand in my life in the past. Help me to expect your intervention in my circumstance by faith. Overshadow me by your grace as I move through the "valley of the shadow of debt." Bring me out into a place of abundance, In Jesus' name. Amen.

CHAPTER 37

STUBBORNNESS

"Listen to me, O my people, while I give you stern
warnings. O Israel, if you will only listen! You must
never worship any other god, nor ever have an idol in
your home. But no, my people won't listen. Israel doesn't
want me around. So, I am letting them go their blind and
stubborn way, living according to their own desires."

Psalm 81:8-9, 11-12

The children of Israel missed out on God's promises because of their stubbornness. Despite repeated warnings against idolatry, the Israelites had a penchant for lusting after strange gods. The bible says we cannot continue in sin and say that grace should abound (Romans 6:1). Their negative attitude towards God would cause them untold misery.

Later in the same psalm, God showed the Israelites what their lives would have been like had they listened to him:

(a) They would have had victory over their enemies through God's help.

(b) Those who hated the Lord would have submitted to him, and Israel would have enjoyed a long time of dominion.

(c) God would have fed the Israelites with the finest of wheat; and satisfied them with honey out of the flinty rock (Psalm 81:13-16).

The children of Israel were not enjoying these benefits at the time this psalm was penned, because they chose to continue in their waywardness. Stubbornness is a major hindrance to overflow. If we are faithful in little, God will make us ruler over much (Matthew 25:21). If we choose to hold on to whatever we have, and are not obeying the commandment to give, we might find ourselves in a dry place of lack and need. We cannot serve God and mammon. We must choose one.

Questions for Reflection

1. Is it possible to make one's job a god?
2. The love of money is the root of all kinds of evil (I Timothy 6:10). How can you tell if you have the 'love of money'? (Hint: Are you able to give freely?)
3. How do you break free from the love of money? (Hint: Do you give to God first and trust him to bless the rest?)
4. Why do we find it difficult to give freely? (Hint: Do you have the fear of lack?)
5. How can we break the fear of lack? (Hint: Psalm 23:1).
6. Do you know that if you had the faith to be born again and to trust Jesus with your life, you already have the measure of faith needed to trust him with your finances?

Meditation

*Command those who are rich in this present age not to be haughty, nor to trust in uncertain riches but in the living God, who gives us richly all things to enjoy. Let them do good, that they be rich in good works, **ready to give, willing to share**, storing up for themselves a good foundation for the time to come, that they may lay hold on eternal life.*

–1 Timothy 6:17-19

Memory Verse

Jesus said to him, "If you want to be perfect, go, sell what you have and give to the poor, and you will have treasure in heaven; and come, follow me." But when the young man heard that saying, he went away sorrowful, for he had great possessions.

--Matthew 19:21-22

Prayer

I love you, Jesus, I love you, Jesus;
I love you, Jesus, I love you.
I love you more than gold;
I love you more than silver.
I love you, Jesus, I love you. (Anonymous)
Lord, let my love for you surpass my love for every other thing. Amen.

CHAPTER 38

ARROGANCE

*"I am the Lord your God, who teaches you **to profit**, who leads you by the way you should go. Oh, that you had heeded my commandments! Then your peace would have been like a river, and your righteousness like the waves of the sea.*

Isaiah 48:17-18 KJV

*"I am God, your God, who teaches you how to live right and well. I show you what to do, where to go. If you had listened all along to what I told you, **your life would have flowed full like a river, blessings rolling in like waves from the sea.***

Isaiah 48:17-18 MSG

God wanted to teach the children of Israel how to profit, but they did not listen to him. They thought they had it all figured out. They forgot the injunction from the bible:

Trust in the Lord with all your heart, and lean not on your under-standing, in all your ways acknowledge him, and he shall direct your paths.

--Proverbs 3:5-6

By refusing God's counsel, the Israelites again missed out on living a good life and experiencing overflow. The profit that God had in mind for them, would have become a generational blessing that they could pass to their descendants. The children of Israel were too proud to submit to God, and acknowledge him as the source of their blessings; therefore, they ended up in the Babylonian captivity and served their enemies.

God has a plan for our prosperity, but we need to find it. There are many pointers that God could use to lead us to the place of blessing. There are hidden riches in secret places that God could reveal to us. God could give us innovative ideas and witty inventions. However, we would not be able to receive the information if we do not seek him closely. If we follow the Lord one step at a time, we will eventually end up in a place of enlargement.

Questions for Reflection

1. Do you believe that God has a personal plan for your prosperity? (Hint: Jeremiah 29:11).
2. Call upon me, and I will show you things which you know not (Jeremiah 33:3). Do you believe that God can show you what you are supposed to do if you ask him?
3. Why have you not asked?
4. How do you plan to do so in the next few days or weeks?
5. Do you believe you already know what God wants you to do?
6. Have you started doing it?
7. What obstacles are hindering you from doing it?

Take the first step of faith, and the Jordan will part before you. Amen.

Meditation

I, wisdom, dwell with prudence, and find out knowledge and discretion. The fear of the Lord is to hate evil; **pride and arrogance** *and the evil way and the perverse mouth I hate.*

--Proverbs 8 12-13

Memory Verse

Commit your works to the Lord, and your plans will succeed.

--Proverbs 16:3 (AMP)

Prayer

Dear Lord,
I believe. Help my unbelief! (Mark 9:24). Help me to trust you as you lead me in the path of prosperity. Help me to find the pathway to my blessings. Amen.

PART VIII

THE THREE GIFTS OF MERCY

God in his mercy has made provision for us to retrace our steps after we have gone in the wrong direction. Even if we have not been diligent in our giving habits, God can give us a second chance or third, and up to infinity. He has given a permanent solution to our sin problem through the death of Jesus Christ. Whenever we sin, even as Christians, we have continual cleansing when we repent and confess our shortcomings (1 John 1:7). He also gives us the grace to do the right thing, and he eventually orders our steps back into what should have been ours. He restores our fortunes. We will unwrap his gifts of mercy in the next series of devotionals.

CHAPTER 39
THE GIFT OF REPENTANCE

*"But go and learn what this means: 'I desire
mercy and not sacrifice. For I did not come to call
the righteous, but sinners, to repentance."*

Matthew 9:13

I f you realized that you have somehow contributed to the lack of overflow in your life by your own mistakes, or omissions, there is still hope for you; there is room for repentance. Repentance is the gift God gave us for the remission of sins. First you need to confess as sin, whatsoever the Holy Spirit might have highlighted that you were doing wrong, which gave the enemy a roadway into your finances. This is also the time to pray and repent of generational alliances with the spirit of mammon.

After confession and repentance, God will extend his forgiveness to you, and put a stop to the negative process that started in your life, because of the sin.

If we say that we have no sin, we deceive ourselves, and the truth is not in us. If we confess our sins, he is faithful and just to forgive us our sins, and to cleanse us from all unrighteousness.

--1 John: 1: 8-9

Having received forgiveness for your shortcomings, God expects you to now live your life in a way that is consistent with your repentance. He expects you to begin doing the right thing. If for instance, you used to give God the remnant of your income after paying all other bills, you need to change your ways. Ask for forgiveness, and begin to give to God first, before paying others. Consequently, the curse on your finances will be broken and you will begin to enjoy God's favor and blessing until you start overflowing with his goodness. Amen.

Questions for Reflection

1. What hindrances to overflow did the Holy Spirit highlight to you as you read the last few chapters?
2. Are they sins of omission such as withholding the tithe, or some of the tithe?
3. Are they generational strongholds? Did you notice the trend of constant financial shortage in your family?
4. Are you guilty of negative talk or lack of faith?
5. Are you willing to repent and change your ways?

Begin to do the right thing. As you remove the hindrances, you will begin to see God's blessings flow into your life.

*** To remove hindrance number 3 above, you need prayers of deliverance, and a total departure from any form of idolatry.

Meditation

Now I rejoice, not that you were made sorry, but that your sorrow led to repentance. For you were made sorry in a godly manner, that you might suffer loss from us in nothing. For godly sorrow produces repentance leading to salvation, not to be regretted; but the sorrow of the world produces death.

--2 Corinthians 7: 9-10

Memory Verse

As a father has compassion on his children, so the Lord has compassion on those who fear him.

--(Psalm 103:13)

Prayer

Dear Lord,

Thank you for your power to cleanse, forgive and deliver me from anything, habit, or powers that hinder me from experiencing your overflowing blessings in my life. I confess and repent of my sins. I trust you to forgive me and place my feet on the path of righteousness. Amen.

CHAPTER 40

THE GIFT OF GRACE

*And of his fullness we have all
received, and grace for grace.*

John 1:16

*And God is able to make all grace abound toward
you; that ye, always having all sufficiency in
all things, may abound to every good work.*

2 Corinthians 9:8

Jesus' arrival on the earth signaled the beginning of a new era for mankind -- the era of grace. God is gracious and plenteous in mercy; he revealed his gift of grace to us through Jesus Christ, his Son. Grace is the divine enablement that helps us to do things that we otherwise would have been unable to do. It helps us to be willing to live our lives in a way that pleases God at every level. After repentance and turning away from our sin, we enter the next stage of bringing forth the fruits worthy of our repentance. We will require the grace of God to bring this to pass.

One aspect of our Christian walk where this grace is needed is in giving. As we discussed in the previous chapters, failure to give is a major reason for lack and shortage in our finances. Paul admonished the Corinthians to give towards the needs of other Christians who were suffering from famine. This kind of giving goes beyond regular tithes and offering, it is a special and additional offering. Therefore, Paul prayed for them that the grace to give will be released abundantly.

He prayed for them that God will bless them so much that they will not give out of lack, but of abundance. They will also have something left over after they might have given (2 Corinthians 9:8). This is how the grace of giving operates; when you decide to be a blessing to the body of Christ, God increases his blessings on your life so that you can continue to give to kingdom causes. The more you give, the more blessings are added to you, and the more you have to share with others.

Questions for Reflection

1. What does grace mean to you?
2. Have you ever experienced the grace of God?
3. Do you remember a time when you had no power to do something and God gave you the grace to do it?
4. Do you believe that you can rely on God's grace and mercy to help you do what you could not do before?
5. If you made a pledge or vow in the past that you did not keep because you could not, do you believe you will now receive grace to pay your vow?
6. If you did not want to tithe your income because you were not willing, do you trust that you will now receive grace to yield to the Holy Spirit and pay your tithe with rejoicing?

Meditation

For by grace you have been saved through faith, and that not of yourselves; it is the gift of God, not of works, lest anyone should boast.

--Ephesians 2:8-9

Memory Verse

For it is God who works in you both to will and to do for his good pleasure.

--Philippians 2:13

Prayer

Lord Jesus,

    I thank you for your grace that saved me from my sins. I thank you for your grace that enables me to please you. Father, let me not take your grace in vain. I receive the 'grace for giving' in abundance today and forever. In Jesus name. Amen.

CHAPTER 41

THE GIFT OF RESTORATION

He restores my soul; he leads me in the paths
of righteousness for his name's sake.

Psalm 23:3

Jesus Christ is our great shepherd. He made provision for our restoration even before we sinned. The bible says that while we were yet sinners Christ died for us (Romans 5:8). After receiving the gift of repentance and grace, we are now positioned for the gift of restoration. God brings restoration to our soul and our spirit. Prosperity is God's will for our lives.

Beloved, I wish above all things that you prosper and be in health, even as your soul prospers.

--3 John:1

God in his mercy leads us back to the path of blessedness; he rearranges our lives such that we begin to flourish and prosper again. Everything the enemy stole from us is restored.

> *The thief does not come except to steal, and to kill, and to destroy. I have come that they may have life, and that they may have it more abundantly*
>
> --John 10:10

If we stay committed to doing the will of God concerning our substance, the Lord will block all the avenues of theft that the enemy had been using against us. He will give us divine health, and then, empower us to get wealth. We will begin to experience overflow in every area of our lives. Amen.

Questions for Reflection

1. Do you think that you need restoration in your life?
2. Do you need restoration in your finances?
3. Can you identify what the enemy stole from you?
4. Do you believe that God can restore what was lost?
5. Do you believe that it is God's will for your stolen property to be restored?
6. When God restores, he gives us multiple folds of what was lost. Expect restoration. It is your portion.

Meditation

So, David inquired of the Lord, saying, "Shall I pursue this troop? Shall I overtake them?"

And he answered him, "Pursue, for you shall surely overtake them and without fail recover all.

---I Samuel 30:8

Memory Verse

For the scepter of wickedness shall not rest on the land allotted to the righteous, lest the righteous reach out their hands to iniquity.

--Psalm 125:3

Prayer

Father God,

Thank you for your plan for the restoration of all that the enemy has stolen from me. I receive your promise by faith and I thank you in advance for the restoration of your glory in my life. I bless you Lord. Amen.

PART IX

THE SHOUT OF RESTORATION!!!

But this is a people robbed and plundered; all of them are snared in holes, and they are hidden in prison houses; they are for prey, and no one delivers; for plunder, and no one says, "Restore!"

Isaiah 42:22

I am excited about the next series of devotionals. God has a plan to restore our lost fortunes. God's plan is multilevel---he wants to restore us individually, generationally, as people groups, and as nations.

If my people, which are called by my name, shall humble themselves, and pray, and seek my face, and turn from their wicked ways; then will I hear from heaven, and will forgive their sin, and will heal their land

(2 Chronicles 7:14).

If we find our livelihoods compromised by uncontrollable circumstances, or we see the enemy take advantage of our situation to steal from us, we need to pray and cry out for God to restore that which was stolen. When we humble ourselves, and ask for restoration, he is faithful to hear us, and restore us.We are going to do just that. Shout Restore!!!

CHAPTER 42

THE YEAR OF JUBILEE!

*And you shall consecrate the fiftieth year, and proclaim
liberty throughout all the land to all its inhabitants. It
shall be a Jubilee for you; and each of you shall return to
his possession, and each of you shall return to his family.*

Leviticus 25:10

The children of Israel lived off the land, they were mostly farm-
ers and cattle ranchers. God required them to give their land
a rest every seven years. After seven Sabbaths, in the fiftieth year,
they were to have a work-free year in which the land had a rest, and
everybody who had lost his inheritance could go back, and repos-
sess his land. Also, debts were forgiven and slaves were freed. It was
a year when the Israelites were to be kind to one another, and put
an end to all oppression. It was the year of Jubilee!!!!

Many people will only experience the year of Jubilee once in a
life time. If they were born close to the year of Jubilee, they might

experience it twice. However, Jesus said in Luke 4:18-19, that he came to fulfill the prophecy in Isaiah 61:1-3:

> *"The Spirit of the Lord God is upon me, because the Lord has anointed me to preach good tidings to the poor; He has sent Me to heal the brokenhearted, to proclaim liberty to the captives, and the opening of the prison to those who are bound; to proclaim **the acceptable year of the Lord**, and the day of vengeance of our God; to comfort all who mourn, to console those who mourn in Zion, to give them beauty for ashes, the oil of joy for mourning, the garment of praise for the spirit of heaviness; that they may be called trees of righteousness, the planting of the Lord, that He may be glorified."*

Once we give our lives to Christ, we immediately enter a perpetual Jubilee. Salvation redeems us from the slavery of sin, and sets us free to possess our inheritance, and recover everything that the enemy stole from us. We no longer have to wait 50 years for Jubilee. We can have Jubilee here and now through the shed blood of Jesus Christ. Your time for restoration is now!

Questions for Reflection

1. Jubilee is a gift of grace. The Israelites did not need to do anything to experience Jubilee. What was the only requirement for Jubilee? (Hint: If you are not dead, you qualify for Jubilee.)
2. Salvation is also a gift of grace, we do not have to do anything to be saved. What is the only requirement for salvation? (Hint: Faith in Jesus Christ -- Believe!)
3. Have you noticed a "trend" of financial insufficiency in your lineage?
4. Do you feel bound and restricted from possessing what rightfully belongs to you? You need the Jubilee! Thankfully you do not have to wait 50 years. Jesus has fulfilled the law.
5. Will you cry out for your deliverance?

Begin to experience Jubilee! Enter a debt-free zone financially. Amen.

Meditation

The Lord will open to you His good treasure, the heavens, to give the rain to your land in its season, and to bless all the work of your hand. **You shall lend to many nations, but you shall not borrow.**

--Deuteronomy 28:12

Memory Verse

For you know the grace of our Lord Jesus Christ, that though he was rich, yet for your sakes he became poor, that you through his poverty might become rich.

--2 Corinthians 8:9

Prayer

Dear Lord Jesus,

Thank you for saving me from my sins, and the consequences thereof. I thank you that you became poor that I might be rich. Thank you for breaking the curse of poverty off my life when you hung on the tree. I break every agreement with the spirit of slavery and poverty. I rejoice for my Jubilee in you. Amen.

CHAPTER 43

DOUBLE FOR YOUR TROUBLE!!

*And the LORD restored Job's losses when he
prayed for his friends. Indeed, the LORD gave
Job twice as much as he had before.*

Job 42:10

Job feared God more than anybody in his day. He enjoyed God's
blessings on everything he laid his hand upon so much so that
he became the wealthiest man in his time. The devil got jealous
of the blessings of God on Job's life, and asked for permission to
tempt him so that he could deny God.

Job lost everything he had, but his love and fear of God. His
wife and his friends ridiculed him, but he stood his ground. He
did not deny God, he stood firm to the end. He passed his test!
God was so proud of Job that at the end of his ordeal, God blessed
him and made the enemy pay back twice everything he stole from
Job. Job was rewarded double for his trouble (Isaiah 61: 7 MSG).

The Lord prolonged his life and he lived to enjoy the goodness of God for a very long time.

God is faithful. He will not forget your labor of love to reward it (Hebrews 6:10). Whatsoever you do for the cause of Christ will be richly rewarded. Many of us will never experience the magnitude of loss that Job had to endure. Even then, whatever the enemy has stolen from you, whether materially, emotionally, or in time and relationships, God will order him to pay you back in multiple folds. He is a rewarder of those who diligently seek him (Hebrews 11:6).

Questions for Reflection

1. Why did God bless Job?
2. Did Job serve God for what he could get from God?
3. Did Job serve God because he loved God?
4. What was the devil's accusation against Job?
5. What was the proof that the enemy was wrong?
6. Did God preserve Job amid the trial?
7. Did God restore Job's lost fortunes?
8. Have you lost something of value to you? Cheer up! Restoration is on the way!

Meditation

People do not despise a thief if he steals to satisfy himself when he is starving. Yet when he is found, he must restore sevenfold; He may have to give up all the substance of his house. --Proverbs 6:30-31

Memory Verse

Because you got a double dose of trouble and more than your share of contempt, your inheritance in the land will be doubled and your joy go on forever.

--Isaiah 61:7 (MSG)

Prayer

Dear Lord,
I thank you again for the opportunity to have my stolen property restored. I place a demand on the enemy, and I call forth everything that was stolen from my generations, from me and from my children. I take it back by the power in the name of Jesus. Amen.

CHAPTER 44

SHOUTS OF JOY!!!

When the Lord brought back the captivity of Zion,
we were like those who dream. Then our mouth
was filled with laughter, and our tongue with
singing. Then they said among the nations, "The
Lord has done great things for them." The Lord
has done great things for us, and we are glad.

Psalm 126:1-3

The Israelites had been in exile in Babylon for 70 long years. When they were in captivity, they could not access their fortunes, nor their inheritance. Whenever they thought of lost opportunities, they would long for home and get depressed.

For there, those who carried us away captive asked of us a song,
And those who plundered us requested mirth,

Saying, "Sing us one of the songs of Zion!"
How shall we sing the Lord's song in a foreign land?

(Psalm 137:3-4)

At the end of 70 years, the Lord raised up a Persian king who facilitated the return of the Jewish exiles to Jerusalem. The first thing that happened after their release was that their joy was restored. Then the nations that used to mock them saw them rejoicing, and testified that God had visited his people. Joy is the hallmark of restoration! The bible says that the joy of the Lord is our strength (Nehemiah 8:32). We need the joy of the Lord in our inner man so that we can possess our inheritance in the land of the living.

God wants to turn around our captivity regardless of the reason for our plight. Maybe it was our own sins, or generational sins. When we confess, and renounce all sins we begin to experience restoration in places that were desolate in our lives. We will begin to reap with joy in the places of our tears, and we will rejoice greatly when our fortunes are restored!

Questions for Reflection

1. Have you ever been depressed?
2. What was the cause of the depression?
3. Have you or someone you know been depressed because of lack and shortage?
4. How did you come out of that depression?
5. Were you happy when the financial oppression was lifted?
6. Are you currently depressed because of poverty?
7. Will you ask for the Lord to restore your fortunes? *Whatsoever he tells you to do, do it* (John 2:5).

Meditation

Shouts of joy and victory resound in the tents of the righteous: "The LORD's right hand has done mighty things!" Save now, I pray, O Lord; O Lord, I pray, send now prosperity.

--Psalm 118:15 & 25

Memory Verse

But on Mount Zion there shall be deliverance, and there shall be holiness; the house of Jacob shall possess their possessions.

--Obadiah 17

Prayer

Lord Jesus,

I come to you just as I am. Heal me of every financial wound that has caused me pain and depression. I break every agreement with the spirit of depression. I choose joy. I choose to rejoice by faith in anticipation of your manifest blessings in my life. Amen.

CHAPTER 45

LOST YEARS RESTORED!!!!

The threshing floors shall be full of wheat, and the vats shall overflow with new wine and oil. "So, I will restore to you the years that the swarming locust has eaten, the crawling locust, the consuming locust, and the chewing locust, my great army which I sent among you."

Joel 2:24-25

The nation of Israel experienced a severe famine due to locust invasion. According to the above verse, God sent the locusts to get their attention. They had been going their rebellious ways, while expecting God to bless them in their disobedience. God got their attention! The priests cried out to God in repentance. The priests and the elders of the land asked the whole nation to fast and pray and repent before the Lord. The Lord in his grace and mercy, heard their prayers and responded with this powerful promise--the restoration of lost years.

If we lose our harvest repeatedly, or for many seasons, it becomes difficult to do things at the right time. Without the necessary flow of funds, important matters are put on hold till the following season. If the lost harvest is not quickly and fully recovered, some years might be lost permanently. If you find yourself in this situation, you need to cry out to the Lord in repentance just like the Israelites did. God wants to restore all that was eaten by the devourer.

When God restores lost years, everything you should have done during those years will be done with acceleration. You will find favor and help from God and man. You will win scholarships for college, and bonuses at work. At the end of the day, you will look back and find that everything you thought you lost has been restored. Also, when God restores lost years, your situation will be better that what you would have had, had the locusts not come. The Israelites would go on to experience the promised increase and more. And so can we!

Questions for Reflection

1. Are you experiencing relentless financial losses? If so, the enemy may be attacking you.
2. God can show you why the enemy has access to your money. Continuous and relentless loss is not God's will for you.
3. Seek the Lord in praying and fasting. He will reveal the secret to you, he will show you the way of escape. Amen.

Meditation

The secret things belong to the Lord our God, but those things which are revealed belong to us and to our children forever, that we may do all the words of this law.

--Deuteronomy 29:29

Memory Verse

And when the king asked the woman, she told him. So, the king appointed a certain officer for her, saying, "Restore all that was hers, and all the proceeds of the field from the day that she left the land until now."

--2 Kings 8:6

Prayer

Dear Lord,
You know how I have grieved for the lost years in my life. I now bring every wasted year to you. Please, redeem them. Oh, satisfy me early with your mercy, that I may rejoice and be glad all my days! Make me glad according to the days in which I have been afflicted,

the years in which I have seen evil. Let your work appear to me (your servant), and your glory to my children. And let the beauty of the Lord my God be upon me, and establish the work of my hands for me; Yes, establish the work of my hands (Psalm 90:14-17, paraphrased). *Amen.*

CHAPTER 46
SHOWERS OF BLESSING!!!!!

And I, the Lord, will be their God, and my servant
David a prince among them; I, the Lord, have spoken.
I will make a covenant of peace with them, and cause
wild beasts to cease from the land; and they will dwell
safely in the wilderness and sleep in the woods. I
will make them and the places all around my hill a
blessing; and I will cause showers to come down in
their season; there shall be showers of blessing.

Ezekiel 34:24-26

The children of Israel were exiles in Babylon when God gave them this promise through the prophet Ezekiel. God promised them a new shepherd from David's lineage. We now understand the new shepherd to be Jesus Christ. God also promised to make a covenant of peace with them, which we now know is the New Covenant in Christ. He is the Prince of Peace.

The second part of this promise is the removal of the evil beasts from the land. That refers to the devil and his agents. The enemy must be removed so that we can enjoy the peace that Jesus purchased for us by his blood. Then he gave the promise of rain at the right time, and blessings on every side.

If you feel you have been battered by the enemy, constantly oppressed and pursued by bad breaks. If you feel like an evil force is militating against your blessings, this promise is for you. He whom the Son has set free is free indeed. First, ask Jesus to become your shepherd. Ask the Lord to remove any generational evil beast that may be operating in your life. Then receive his showers of blessing over you and everything that belongs to you.

Questions for Reflection

1. Are you experiencing peace in your sleep?
2. Are you plagued by nightmares of evil beasts?
3. Do you see wild animals such as snakes, huge angry dogs, or lions in your dreams? These are all evil beasts that want to rob you of your inheritance.
4. Will you accept the reign of the Prince of Peace in your life? Enter into the covenant of peace with Jesus. Command the evil beasts to leave in Jesus' name. Amen.

Meditation

Then it came to pass the seventh time, that he said, "There is a cloud, as small as a man's hand, rising out of the sea!" So, he said, "Go up, say to Ahab, 'Prepare your chariot, and go down before the rain stops you.'" Now it happened in the meantime that the sky became black with clouds and wind, and there was a heavy rain.

(I Kings 18: 44-45b).

Memory Verse

A highway shall be there, and a road and it shall be called the Highway of Holiness. The unclean shall not pass over it, but it shall be for others. Whoever walks the road, although a fool, shall not go astray. No lion shall be there, nor shall any ravenous beast go up on it; it shall not be found there. But the redeemed shall walk there.

--Isaiah 35:8-9

Prayer

Dear Lord,

I thank you that you are my Prince of Peace. Let every evil beast that is hindering my blessings be rebuked in your name. Make my feet like hind's feet so I can walk upon my high places (Habakkuk 3:19). Establish your blessings in my life and my lineage. Amen.

PART X
EVIDENCE OF OVERFLOW

We have seen throughout this book how God wants to bless us extravagantly. We have also studied many promises in the Bible to that effect. Is it possible for us to bless God in return, in the same manner with which he has blessed us? Can we respond to God in exuberance? Can we make blessings overflow back to God? What will be his response to us? We will find out in these last series of devotionals as we explore: The Evidence of Overflow.

CHAPTER 47

ABEL'S OFFERING

Abel also brought of the firstborn of his flock and of their
fat. And the Lord respected Abel and his offering.

Genesis. 4:4

C ain and Abel were Adam and Eve's children. When they grew
up, they chose different occupations. Cain became a farmer
while Abel chose to be a shepherd. They both gave to the Lord
from the proceeds of the work of their hands. Abel gave God the
first and the best of his increase. His offering touched God's heart,
and was accepted by the Lord.

By faith Abel offered to God a more excellent sacrifice than Cain,
through which he obtained witness that he was righteous, God testi-
fying of his gifts; and through it he being dead still speaks

(Hebrews 11:4).

Unfortunately, Cain had given God an unacceptable offering. He got jealous of his brother Abel and killed him in the field. Even in death, three things happened to Abel because he gave God his best.

(a) God testified of Abel's gifts.
(b) Abel's offering witnessed to his righteousness.
(c) Abel's offering vindicated him in death.

God always takes note of our motive in giving to him. When we give him our best, he responds to our gesture by accepting our sacrifice. He boasts about our offering and devotion to him. Our offerings will continue to speak for us in God's presence long after we might have given the gift. When we get into trouble God will remember our offerings, and help us out.

> *May the Lord answer you in the day of trouble; May the name of the God of Jacob defend you; May he send you help from the sanctuary, and strengthen you out of Zion;* ***May he remember all your offerings, and accept your burnt sacrifice***

(Psalm 20:1-3).

Long after we are dead, God will still remember our offerings. He will bless our descendants because of our offerings. Amen.

Questions for Reflection

1. How does it feel for you to know that God personally receives your offering as a sacrifice with sweet-smelling savor?
2. Do you know that the offerings you give to God are recorded in heaven?
3. Do you understand the concept that your offering has a voice?
4. Do you believe that when you give an offering, you are not the only one giving, but you and your children and generations yet to come through you?
5. Now that you know, will that change the way you give?
6. Now that you know, will you give with greater expectation of God's blessing, not only on you, but on your descendants?

Meditation

Even Levi, who receives tithes, paid tithes through Abraham, so to speak, for he was still in the loins of his father when Melchizedek met him.

--Hebrews 7: 9-10

Memory Verse

A good man leaves an inheritance to his children's children, but the wealth of the sinner is stored up for the righteous.

--Proverbs 13:22

Prayer

Dear Lord,
    I ask for forgiveness for my nonchalant attitude about giving to you. Create in me a new heart, renew a right spirit within me. Help me to treat my gifts to you as holy and sacred. Thank you for your promise of generational blessings on my descendants. Amen.

CHAPTER 48

THE OFFERING IN THE WILDERNESS

And they spoke to Moses, saying, "The people bring much more than enough for the service of the work which the Lord commanded us to do." So, Moses gave a commandment, and they caused it to be proclaimed throughout the camp, saying, "Let neither man nor woman do any more work for the offering of the sanctuary." And the people were restrained from bringing.

Exodus 36:5-6

When the Israelites left the nation of Egypt, the Lord led them to ask for jewelry from the Egyptians; the Lord granted them favor in the sight of the Egyptians, they gave their jewelry to the Israelites. The Israelites thereby plundered the nation of Egypt. The nation of Israel in the wilderness was a wealthy nation. God had blessed them with great substance. The Lord requested a tabernacle to be built for him in the wilderness. He also asked Moses to ask the children of Israel for the building materials (Exodus 35:5-9).

The children of Israel responded to the call with enthusiasm, they gave so much that the workers told Moses to stop the people from bringing any more offerings.

> *Then all the craftsmen who were doing all the work of the sanctuary came, each from the work he was doing, and they spoke to Moses, saying, "The people bring much more than enough for the service of the work which the Lord commanded us to do. And the people were restrained from bringing, for the material they had was sufficient for all the work to be done—indeed too much.*

(Exodus 36:4-5, & 7).

The Lord was pleased with their sacrifice. When the tabernacle was finally finished, the glory of God showed up!

> *Then the cloud covered the tent of meeting, and the glory of the Lord filled the tabernacle. Moses could not enter the tent of meeting because the cloud had settled on it, and the glory of the Lord filled the tabernacle.*

(Exodus 40:34-35).

The Lord would henceforth lead them by the presence of the cloud on the tabernacle. When the cloud rested on the tabernacle, they stayed in the place, and when the cloud moved, they continued their journey (Exodus 40:36-37). When we honor God with our substance, he tabernacles with us and orders our steps in the paths of prosperity. Amen.

Questions for Reflection

1. God restored Israel's lost fortunes in 24 hours! He turned them from being a group of slaves with no income to a wealthy nation. Do you believe he can do the same for you?
2. There was a primary purpose for this blessing that God gave them, so that they could build God's house and keep the overflow for their use. Did the Israelites fulfill that primary purpose?
3. What was God's response to their excessive (undue) offering?
4. Have you ever given God an undue offering? (Abundant offering out of your abundance)? If you have not, get ready. He will soon give you the opportunity to do so.

Meditation

The glory of the Lord shall be revealed, and all flesh shall see it together; for the mouth of the Lord has spoken.

--Isaiah 40:5

Memory Verse

The steps of a good man are ordered by the Lord, and he delights in his way.

--Psalm 37:23

Prayer

Father God,
Thank you for your abundant gifts overflowing in my life. Help me to be a faithful steward of all that I have received. As I

give to you from the abundance you have given me, let me continue to enjoy your presence and guidance. In Jesus' name, I pray. Amen.

CHAPTER 49
A THOUSAND BURNT OFFERINGS

*Now the king went to Gibeon to sacrifice there, for
that was the great high place: Solomon offered a
thousand burnt offerings on that altar. At Gibeon,
the Lord appeared to Solomon in a dream by night;
and God said, "Ask! What shall I give you?"*

I Kings 3:4-5

The young Solomon started his reign as the third king of Israel by giving God a thousand burnt offerings. That means a thousand animals were killed and prepared specially to be burnt as offerings unto the Lord. He got God's attention! God visited Solomon in a dream at night, and in response to his unprecedented offering, God allowed Solomon to ask for whatever he wanted (an open check). Solomon asked for wisdom, but in addition to wisdom God gave him an overflow of every good thing in life: wealth, honor, and dominion.

That was not the only time Solomon gave such extravagant (undue) offerings. At the dedication of the temple that Solomon built for the Lord, he had the priests sacrifice thousands of all manner of offerings before the Lord on the altar of sacrifice. The altar was too small for the sacrifices, so Solomon dedicated the center court of the temple for offering sacrifices. I wonder how long it took them to offer all the animals. What happened next is mind boggling:

> *When Solomon had finished praying,* **fire came down from heaven** *and consumed the burnt offering and the sacrifices; and the glory of the Lord filled the temple. And the priests could not enter the house of the Lord, because the glory of the Lord had filled the Lord's house*

(2 Chronicles 7:1-2).

Giving to God is an act of worship. When we worship God with a pure heart and give to him largely and lavishly, there is no telling how he will respond to our worship. We might get open checks, glory clouds, and even fire!

Questions for Reflection

1. Solomon gave an unprecedented offering to God. The bible does not clearly state prior to that time that someone had given God a thousand offerings. Would you like to be the first in your lineage to give God such an offering?
2. Solomon's gifts literally opened the windows of heaven for Solomon. He had dreams and visions. Can God do the same for you?
3. Do you believe in dreams and visions?
4. God used dreams and visions to guide Jacob, Isaac, Solomon and Daniel into their prosperity. Can he do the same for you?
5. Are you willing to experience God at this level?
6. You may not see a physical glory cloud, but God's glory can rest on you -- manifesting as favor with God and man. Do you want that glory?

Meditation

And Jesus increased in wisdom and stature, and in favor with God and men.

--Luke 2:52

Memory Verse

For the Lord God is a sun and shield; The Lord will give grace and glory; No good thing will He withhold from those who walk uprightly.

–Psalm 84:11

Prayer

Dear Lord,
    Bless me and make me a blessing. Use me for the expansion of your kingdom. Let my offerings bring you pleasure. Manifest your glory in my life. Amen.

CHAPTER 50

MARY'S LOVE OFFERING

And behold, a woman in the city who was a sinner,
when she knew that Jesus sat at the table in the
Pharisee's house, brought an alabaster flask of fragrant
oil, and stood at His feet behind Him weeping; and
she began to wash His feet with her tears, and wiped
them with the hair of her head; and she kissed His
feet and anointed them with the fragrant oil.

Luke 7:38-39

There was a certain sinner woman who experienced Jesus' pardon and forgiveness. She brought her alabaster box of ointment and freely and unashamedly poured out her love on Jesus. The bible later revealed that this woman was Mary, the sister of Lazarus (John 11:2).

The Pharisees were not happy that Jesus allowed a sinner to anoint him. Jesus explained to them that Mary had been forgiven much and therefore she loved much (Luke 7:47). Jesus testified of her love for him and he was pleased with her offering. Mary was unwavering in her love for Jesus, she would later anoint him again from her alabaster box, but the second time, the bible revealed the cost of the perfume; 300 denarii, a whole year's worth in wages! (Mark 14:5, John 12:5 NIV). She lavished it on Jesus.

Again, the people around were indignant. "Why should she waste so much money on Jesus?" She could have put the money to better use. Jesus rebuked the naysayers. He told them that Mary had anointed him for his burial, and therefore anywhere the gospel is preached, her name will be mentioned (Mathew 14:8-9). What a great honor! Are we willing to give to God even when we are ridiculed for our giving? Are we willing to lavish our love on him? How about giving a whole year's salary? That would cause no little stir. But it would also cause some astronomical rewards. Jesus wants our love first. Then all our gifts, large or small, will be acceptable in his sight.

Questions for Reflection

1. Mary's gift was a classic case of (undue) excessive, extravagant, lavish overflow unto the Lord. It got the critics' attention. Are you willing to give God a gift that will draw the ire of your critics?
2. Have you broken your alabaster box to give God something very precious to you?
3. How would it feel to give God a whole year's worth of wages?
4. When Mary did this, she did not know that her brother will fall sick. Her gift went into her future to secure her brother's restoration to life. Do you know what your extravagant gift might be preserving in your future?
5. Mary could give from her heart because she had experienced forgiveness and salvation from the Lord. Have you asked for the forgiveness of your sins so that you can be saved?

TODAY is the day of salvation!

Meditation

How shall we escape if we neglect so great a salvation, which at the first began to be spoken by the Lord, and was confirmed to us by those who heard him?

--Hebrews 2:3

Memory Verse

But God demonstrates his own love toward us, in that while we were still sinners, Christ died for us.

--Romans 5:8

Prayer

Dear Lord Jesus,
    Make me a person after your own heart. Help me to love you with all my heart, with all my soul, and with all my might. Amen.

CHAPTER 51
JESUS' ULTIMATE OFFERING

There is a fountain filled with blood
drawn from Emmanuel's veins;
And sinners plunged beneath that
flood lose all their guilty stains.
Lose all their guilty stains, lose all their guilty stains;
And sinners plunged beneath that
flood lose all their guilty stains.

William Cowper

Jesus is our Passover Lamb. Just as a lamb was sacrificed for the sins of the children of Israel once in a year, so was Jesus sacrificed for our sins once and for all. He is the ultimate offering. Salvation is free but it cost God his only begotten Son, and it caused Jesus Christ his life--- but thank God, the grave could not hold him! Hallelujah!!!!

The shedding of the blood of Jesus at Calvary paid the price for our sins. The blood of Jesus is still flowing fresh. It is an overflowing, ever-flowing fountain of love for the cleansing of the guilty.

According to the law, all things are purified with blood; and without shedding of blood there is no remission

(Hebrews 9:22).

We cannot fully partake of the promises of overflowing blessings, except we are part of the blood covenant. When we accept Jesus as our Lord and Savior, we are free from the effects of sin, generational curses, and the grip of the enemy. We are free to pursue our destiny to reign as kings and priests in life (I Peter 2:9, Revelation 1:6).

Therefore, if the Son makes you free, you shall be free indeed

(John 8:36).

Questions for Reflection

1. Are you born again?
2. Jesus explained to Nicodemus in John chapter 3 that unless a man be born again, he cannot see the kingdom of God. What does it mean to be born again?

    The bible states that if anyone is in Christ, he is a new creation; old things have passed away; and all things have become new (2 Corinthians 5:17). When you accept Jesus into your life by believing in Jesus Christ as the Savior that was slain, and resurrected on the third day for the remission of your sins, you become born again, you become new.
3. If you have read this book up till this point, and you are yet to give your life to Christ, this is your opportunity to receive him into your heart. Do not postpone the day of your salvation. Will you accept Jesus Christ as your Lord and Savior today?

God bless you as you do so. Amen.

Meditation

That if you confess with your mouth the Lord Jesus and believe in your heart that God has raised him from the dead, you will be saved.

--Romans 10:9

Memory Verse

For God so loved the world that he gave his only begotten Son, that whoever believes in him should not perish but have everlasting life.

--John 3:16

Prayer

Dear Lord Jesus,

Thank you for saving me. I choose to accept you today as my Lord and Savior. I acknowledge and repent of my sins. I thank you for your death on the cross. I thank you that you died for me. I receive your forgiveness and a new lease of life in you. I thank you that I am born again Amen.

CHAPTER 52

THE EARLY CHURCH'S RADICAL OFFERING

Nor was there anyone among them who lacked; for all who were possessors of lands or houses sold them, and brought the proceeds of the things that were sold, and laid them at the apostles' feet; and they distributed to each as anyone had need.

Acts 4:34-35

The early church took the concept of giving to a higher level. All the believers had everything in common, and nobody lacked anything. No wonder they experienced such great signs and wonders! The wealthy believers sold their possessions so that other believers could be provided for. That goes beyond the level of tithes, offerings and first fruits. That is giving sacrificially and in love which is the type of offering God honors.

Through the giving lifestyle of the early church, the Holy Spirit revealed the purpose for overflow. The purpose of overflow is for the furtherance of the gospel of our Lord and Savior Jesus Christ. God wants to bring us into the overflow not to consume our abundance on our lusts, but so that we are able to meet our own needs, and always have more than enough left over for the needs of others and the spread of the gospel.

If we are broke and always in poverty and lack, always trying to make ends meet, we will never be able to give towards the furtherance of the gospel, to missionaries, orphanages, prisons, and other ventures that God may choose for us. Therefore, God wants to free us from financial bondage, so that we can serve him in liberty. God is searching for Christian financiers who would give thousands, millions, and billions of dollars (and other currencies as applicable), to the work of the end time harvest of souls into the kingdom of God. Will you be one of them?

Questions for Reflection

1. Would you like to be among those that God is preparing to finance the end time harvest?
2. Will you prepare yourself to be used of God in this capacity?
3. If you faithfully practice what you have learnt in this book, you will go from one level of glory to the next, until you break out into the promised overflow that God has for you. Amen.

Meditation

But in a great house there are not only vessels of gold and silver, but also of wood and clay, some for honor and some for dishonor. Therefore, if anyone cleanses himself from the latter, he will be a vessel for honor, sanctified and useful for the Master, prepared for every good work.

--2 Timothy 2: 0-212

Memory Verse

But seek first the kingdom of God and his righteousness, and all these things shall be added to you.

-- Matthew 6:33

Prayer

And God is able to make all grace [every favor and earthly bless-ing] come in abundance to you, so that you may always [under all circumstances, regardless of the need] have complete sufficiency in everything [being completely self-sufficient in Him], and have an abundance for every good work and act of charity. As it is written and forever remains written,

He [the benevolent and generous person] scattered abroad, he gave to the poor,

His righteousness endures forever!

Now he who provides seed for the sower and bread for food will provide and multiply your seed for sowing [that is, your resources] and increase the harvest of your righteousness [which shows itself in active goodness, kindness, and love]. You will be enriched in every way so that you may be generous, and this [generosity, administered] through us is producing thanksgiving to God [from those who benefit]. For the ministry of this service (offering) is not only supplying the needs of the saints (God's people), but is also overflowing through many expressions of thanksgiving to God (2 Corinthians 9:8-12 AMP). *Amen.*

God bless you!

ABOUT THE AUTHOR

 Author Rebekah Kassim has written two Christian devotionals for women. One, *Devotionals for Pregnant Women*, won the Choice Books award for best devotional in Spring 2009.

Rebekah is currently a doctoral student at Liberty University, Virginia. She previously received her master's degree in Zoology from the University of Ibadan in Nigeria. She and her husband, Mark, live in Northern Virginia. They are blessed with five children.

Made in the USA
Middletown, DE
24 January 2018